SMELL THE BLUE SKY
ENHANCED VERSION

VALERIE IHSAN

Smell the Blue Sky

ENHANCED edition

SMELL THE BLUE SKY

YOUNG, PREGNANT, AND WIDOWED

Valerie Ihsan

WILLOW BENCH BOOKS
SPRINGFIELD, OREGON

Smell the Blue Sky: young, pregnant and widowed ENHANCED edition

© 2018 Valerie Ihsan

All rights reserved. This book or any portion thereof may not be reproduced or used in any manner whatsoever without the express written permission of the publisher, except for the use of brief quotations in a book review.

Cover Design: paperandsage.com

Willow Bench Books

796 Kelly Blvd

Springfield, OR 97477

Valerie@valerieihsanauthor.com

ISBN: 978-0-9975810-7-2

Library of Congress Control Number: 2018901267

OTHER BOOKS BY VALERIE IHSAN

Fiction

The Scent of Apple Tea

Non-Fiction

Smell the Blue Sky: Young, pregnant, and widowed

How to Grieve: Even when you don't want to

FREE BOOK OFFER

Early Reviews for *The Scent of Apple Tea*
"The story grabbed me right away."
"...a beautiful, very touching and realistic characterization of the mother/daughter bond."
"I loved the ending."
"...beautiful, poignant and very meaningful."
"...fun reading and great local flavor."

Family. Courage. Love.
Kathryn Gordon's cozy rural life falls apart when her adult daughter, Heather, is diagnosed with ovarian cancer. While Kathryn researches alternative cures, including communicating with a dead Scottish ancestor, Heather Gordon makes a heroic journey to Scotland with an ex-boyfriend she still loves.

The Scent of Apple Tea is a story of wanting what you can't have, and finding the courage to live and love the life you're given. If you like reading about strong female protagonists and scenic foreign lands, you'll love Valerie Ihsan's debut contemporary women's fiction novel.

Transport yourself today to the quaint farmlands of Oregon's Willamette Valley and the lush lochs and villages of the Scottish Highlands.

"A lyrical, deep and emotional story; the dynamic...will pull you in and make you think about your own relationships." —Kristen James, *All in My Head*

Go to <u>valerieihsanauthor.com</u> to claim your free book.

In loving memory ...
Robert Joseph Gomes-Pereira
5/25/1972 – 8/17/2000

Thank you, thank you, thank you
For being crazy in love with me,
For our children,
And for your tenderness.
I will always remember you.

∼

And to Paul,
Who maintained his belief in me
And thought I was the awesomest.

∼

To Robert and Clover,
So you will remember.
I love you forever.

Perhaps they are not stars,
  But rather openings in Heaven
  Where the love of our lost ones
  Pours through and shines down upon us
  To let us know they are happy.

(from an Eskimo legend)

Stop all the clocks, cut off the telephone,
    Prevent the dog from barking with a juicy bone,
    Silence the pianos and with muffled drum
    Bring out the coffin, let the mourners come.

Let aeroplanes circle moaning overhead
    Scribbling on the sky the message He Is Dead,
    Put crepe bows round the white necks of the public doves,
    Let the traffic policemen wear black cotton gloves.

He was my North, my South, my East and West,
    My working week and my Sunday rest,
    My noon, my midnight, my talk, my song;
    I thought that love would last forever: I was wrong.

The stars are not wanted now: put out every one;
    Pack up the moon and dismantle the sun;
    Pour away the ocean and sweep up the wood.
    For nothing now can ever come to any good.

~W.H. Auden

THE ANSWER TO EVERYTHING

I'm going to say this right now, up front.

I'm still grieving.

But not in the way you think. We all grieve, after all. About everything. Big griefs and little griefs. You broke your favorite mug, you have a fight with your friend, your mom moves out of the state for a new job.

Right now I am grieving something entirely unrelated to Rob. It *is* about love though. And letting go. Moving on, but not. And that is what the book is about. My love of Rob, letting go of it, moving on, but not.

While writing this book, it never seemed finished. I'd write it, it wouldn't seem right, I'd revise it, it wouldn't seem right, I'd edit it. *Ad nauseum*. And then. When it seemed just about perfect, it wasn't. My friend said that I couldn't finish the book because my universal theme of *letting go, moving on, but not* wasn't happening in my life in the present, so how could I be the expert and show you all how I did it?

Well, here's the secret. The answer to everything.

I *am* the expert. And so are you. You are the expert on your experience, and I am the expert on mine. The expert on grieving Rob's death, how I let go, moved forward, but didn't forget him.

How he's still in my life through our children, in the Portuguese phrases that come without warning to mind, to giggling every time I hear reference to habanera peppers because he burned his penis with pepper oil after cutting up the peppers and then scratching. *Snort, snuffle, swallow. Heehee.* Still gets me every time.

It *did* work – the "letting go, moving on, but not." I'm just going through the process again with someone else. Only without the death this time. Listen, there will always be pre-existing expectations that will need to be let go of. Use this book as a handbook then. A memoirish handbook for letting go, moving on, but not.

I know I will.

AN INTRODUCTION TO MY NAME

My name comes from the Latin *Valerius* – to be strong. In French it means brave. Funny.

I never thought of myself as brave or strong – until now.

My dad did though. He said so one night on the phone after Rob died. I was pacing the New England parlor in the dark while my daughter slept, and my mother-in-law was working second shift at an adult foster care home. (My mother-in-law was strong and brave and valiant. Not me.)

But now I know that I am. I've grown into that strength. Or maybe I had it all along and it only showed up when triggered, like those desert plants that look dead and dry until the rare rains come and they blossom red all in one day, surprising themselves.

I didn't become brave all in one day though. It took months and months, and even then what I did never seemed brave to me. Putting one foot in front of the other every day doesn't seem valiant to me; it's just what you did.

Maybe that's all being brave is. Doing what you *have* to do.

Some days it's all there is.

PART I

Grief Shadows

(Massachusetts)

CHAPTER 1

 *"We've only been apart for about two hours now and I miss the hell out of you. I feel so comfortable with you. I haven't been this happy in a long time..."*
~Rob; love letter excerpt

A doorbell rings through fuzzy sleep and I look at the clock. 1:00 a.m. *Rob?* I flip back the covers and pull on Rob's navy robe. It's closer than mine. I rush down the green shag carpeted hall to the door – sleep still sticking to my eyes. Rob's mom, Fernanda, beats me there. She unbolts the door and we see Rob standing on the other side. *What's he doing here?* He's supposed to be on Cape Cod doing his Annual Training for the National Guard.

He steps through the white screen door that always slams too hard and hugs his mom. The humid summer night clings to his clothes.

"*Aiy!* Why are you here?" Fernanda says.

"I'm here to see you. Just for a little bit, then I need to get back. I missed you." A big smile. White teeth against his dark *"Portagee"* skin, black hair, and sooty lashes.

They embrace warmly. I smile at Rob over Fernanda's shoulder. He smiles back and his eyes speak of tenderness. Fernanda gets one more smooch and pads downstairs to her section of the house. Her feet on the stairs make happy sounds.

Rob and I retire to the bathroom. It's our favorite place to talk. Many heartfelt confessions have been revealed at two or three in the morning in that blue and white tiled bathroom. The noisy and annoying overhead fan is perfect for private conversations. Even though we have our own living space, privacy is still an issue while we live with Rob's mom.

So that's where I tell him that after *eight months of trying*, we finally have Baby Number Two on the way. Our toddler will get her sibling. Rob bounces up and down on the balls of his feet – his knees rigid – and giggles. We hug and cry with relief, excitement and anticipation.

In the kitchen, Rob yawns. I hand him a travel mug for his drive back in our silver Explorer.

"Why go now? It's almost two in the morning. Just stay the night and drive back to the base in a few hours. Sleep now." I pull at his jacket and plead. A forty-five minute visit in the middle of the night – just because – isn't as satisfying as you'd think. He still has a week left of his training.

"I can't. " He smiles knowingly. "I'd never wake up in time for formation."

I droop. He's right. We walk to the door and hug again.

"Drive safe."

"Always," he says. He looks down at me from his additional five inches.

"I love you, " I say.

He walks through the door and as I close it behind him a song from *Alabama*, unbidden, comes to mind. I sway down the dark hall, singing about angels working among us during dark hours of the soul, and climb back in bed smiling. Rob knows. We're pregnant. And our beautiful baby girl is sleeping beside our bed in the crib. Life is wonderful.

THE FIVE A.M. KNOCK AT THE DOOR SENDS FINGERNAILS OF DREAD scratching the blackboard of my mind. Funny how the one a.m. doorbell didn't scare me but the five a.m. knock does. I stumble to the window and see a flashlight beam shining in the dark. Three uniforms appear from the shadows; stiff navy blue fabric hold the men rigid. It is Thursday, August 17, 2000.

"Mrs. Gomes-Pereira?"

"Yes," I say. My lips feel dry; I clutch Rob's robe tighter around me.

"May we come in?"

"Who is it?" Fernanda's voice asks from out of the darkness. She had followed me into the parlor. "Who's here?" she demands in a Portuguese accent.

I feel dazed. *Rob*. I grapple with the screen door lock.

Nothing is said. The silence shouts at me and I watch the somber faces file into the dining room. The face in the back closes the door. The one in front, a mustached man of fifty, holds up a scrap of paper.

"Does Robert Gomes-Pereira live here?"

"Yes," I whisper. My legs betray me and I drop onto the computer chair.

"I don't know how to tell you this, ma'am, but there's been an accident and he didn't make it."

My breath raggles to a stop. I look at each of the three Massachusetts state troopers one at a time. My brain can't take these words and make sense of them. They just float and roll in the waves like soggy driftwood. Through blurry eyes I see Fernanda bend over and stumble, like Grief punched her in the stomach.

"My poor boy. *Meu filho!*" Fernanda wails. She lunges at the telephone receiver and stops. Horror.

"The number! What's the number? Why can't I ... I don't remember ..."

I know she means Gerry's, of course. I recite my sister-in-law's phone number and look over at the green pseudo-suede parlor sofa and the "throne" chair that Rob will never inherit from his mom.

"Do you want us to stay until someone gets here for you?" The mustached trooper steps forward, the forgotten scrap of paper still in his hand.

"My sister-in-law is coming." I see the troopers getting restless, wanting to leave this suffocating haze of grief before them, but I want to know what happened. The two younger men shift their hats and clear their throats.

The man with the mustache is talking again. I look into his apologetic eyes and struggle to understand. He's saying something about the accident. I try to listen but a tiny green fuzz nestled between his shirt collar and neck distracts me.

"It appears he fell asleep driving. He hit an exit signpost on Route 25."

A wave rises from my stomach to my throat. I swallow and shut my eyes. No tears come, but I hear crying. It isn't me; it's Aubrey. I hurry to our bedroom and lift her out of the crib, grateful to escape the nothingness in the parlor.

Aubrey's thick toddler hair is damp from the sweaty room but despite the humidity she clings to me as if scared. Another clunk in my throat. *Can she know already?*

Back in the parlor, Fernanda sobs something and reaches for Aubrey, but she must be frightened of all the tears and sounds coming from her beloved *Vavo*, because Aubrey grasps instead to me. And grateful, I bury my nose deep in her hair and croon softly in her ear until the uniformed faces leave.

Still wearing Rob's robe, I stare at nothing. Somewhere in the back a TV sings inappropriately cheery songs to occupy the innocent Aubrey. Fernanda shuffles back and forth moaning and praying under her breath. I look at the floor. *I have to call my mom.* It's time. I find myself back in my bedroom, a haven of sorts – though you wouldn't think so anymore. I blink at the phone. Sandpaper eyes. My right index finger dials the number. I stare at its ragged cuticle.

This isn't real, I promise myself. The answering machine picks up. It's 2:30 a.m. in Oregon. Should I leave a message? What would I say? *'Hi Mom, Call me back. Rob's dead?'*

I push my fingers into my eyes and take a deep breath.

"Mom? It's Valerie. Are you awake? Wake up. I need to talk to you." I wait, holding my breath, hiding in the dark of our bedroom.

"Hello? Valerie? I couldn't find the phone ..."

"Mom!" I'm so relieved that she's truly there that the word gushes out. "Mom. Rob died this morning -- in a car accident." My throat swells and it feels like something is squishing my esophagus. Darkness burns the edges of my mind, curling them like charred paper. I start to shake and finally a few tears come. But not nearly enough to dislodge the huge boulder pressing at my lungs.

My mom thrives in a crisis. I know this. All my life I've seen her take on a billion tasks at a time and succeed at everything she does. A daunting example to follow, sure, but I know that when I call her, she will know exactly what to do.

I don't really hear anything she says on the phone. Only, "I'll be there. I'll figure it out and call you back in a few hours. I love you."

I drift downstairs and sit on the floor, aching for Aubrey, so beautiful, so oblivious. I ache for Rob, too. *Is he really gone? What am I going to do now?*

I want to grow old with Rob.

We had just received our passports in the mail. We planned to go to France and Germany in the Spring. A sour feeling rises within me, tainting my cells and pores with stink. The European family trip is only one of many dreams that he and I will never realize. Our family is broken.

Where will I go now? Who will I belong to? Where will I fit in?

A door slamming and a flurry of steps interrupt my thoughts. I force my head to turn and I get up from the floor where I'm slumped.

"Mom! Valerie!" *Thud, thud, thud* down the stairs – racing to get to us. Rob's two sisters, Gerry and Lena, burst around the corner. I raise my arms to them and we embrace and lean into each other, seeking comfort. We weep and snuffle and choke, snot and tears smearing together.

And then they turn to their mother.

Gerry is the oldest. She wears fun plastic glasses in trendy styles and hands me buckets of quarters when we visit casino slot machines on special occasions. She blinks when she talks and has a quiet but sing-songy voice. It's pretty fast, too – her voice. And she laughs when she talks. Her laugh is loud and tinkly, like wind-chimes. I love it.

Lena is the middle child. *Was*. Her and Rob, as children, were always together – sought comfort from each other. Were buddies. Lena is self-deprecating and can always make me smile. She smokes – something else she shared with Rob. Me too, actually, until 10 p.m. last night when I found out I was pregnant. No more smoking now though. Not with this little one inside me. I touch my belly with a frantic, yet smoothing, gesture. Lena wears sensible shoes and swimsuits that cover everything up and never lets anyone in her apartment. Not even her mom. I've never seen it. She laughs when she talks, too.

I wonder when any of us will do that again – laugh.

Over the next couple of hours, more family arrives to share condolences and grief. Some bring me comfort and strength where I have none. Some come in an outpouring of grief and I splash into the waves and cry, too. I feel small relief from these tears, though. They are never enough.

My crying strikes me as too dainty, or polite. I want to sob and thrash, to keen and wail. I feel weird and unsettled by it. I suppose I must be in shock, but then I wouldn't *know* I was in shock, would I? Like a crazy person doesn't know he's crazy.

I sit in a folding chair next to the phone downstairs. I'm waiting for State Trooper Brito to call me back and give me any more information about the accident. He found Rob. I'm waiting for the morgue to call me back, too, so we can tell them where to send the body.

Actually, I don't really know why I'm sitting here. I'm just waiting. Waiting to know what to do. Waiting to feel something and conversely to not feel anything. I just stare at the floor and at the phone cord twisting down long, past the red Formica countertops.

Two or three people mill around the kitchen and the boiler room where Fernanda hangs up our clothes to dry in the winter – the ones she doesn't put in the dryer. The rest of the basement room is ringed by family members sitting haggard in chairs. Our life without Rob has barely begun and we already look hollow.

The boiler room beckons.

Maybe someone is hiding in there now. Hiding from the rest of the faces, crying.

When Lena and Gerry first came over, before the rest of the family knew, Lena disappeared out in the backyard for awhile. I imagine what she must've done out there. Pacing in the dewy grass, her hands in fists, punching the air with them and beating her knees and sobbing and then wilting down to the back step and hugging her knees to her chest, trembling, rocking, and smoking a cigarette.

I wish I had the energy to be out there doing the same thing instead of sitting by this phone. But I only seem to be able to sit, with my hands in my lap, or holding my head up. With barely the awareness to breathe. Sometimes I even forget to do that and a cavernous sigh rushes out up from my knees. And then I forget to do it again until the next rush.

It hasn't even been three hours since I've heard of his death – maybe eight since I've seen him last – but I already miss him.

I miss how his eyes half shut and he looks at me underneath his lashes. I miss the sound of his giggle when he gets shy or nervous.

A sad smile tries to lift the corners of my mouth. He giggles like that when I tickle him, too. Or when we have sex. Sometimes he gets all vampire-ish. His eyes flash and sparkle and he gets this evil grin on his face, and then he growls at me. I miss that already, too.

I love it when his eyes fill up with love – sometimes he says, "I love you," and other times he swallows it back. When I see that, my heart melts and I know I'm the most important person in the world.

All my organs sink lower into my body and my blood congeals. *I'm no longer that important person anymore.* Will I ever be? It dawns on me that all those things I miss about Rob, are now things that I *missed* about him. Because he no longer *is*, but *was*. He's now in the past tense. My vision narrows, a black circle compressing my corneas, and I collapse into myself.

Portuguese families are big. They are full of noisy, overbearing, loving and helpful people. I rely on this aid now and lean into it. My favorite of Rob's extended family is his godfather and uncle, Louie. He's here now, wandering from room to room – benevolence and compassion and pain exuding from every neuron. He is calm and charming with twinkling blue eyes. They always hold a joke in them. He reminds me a little of my own uncle.

I was welcomed by all of Rob's family when we moved to Massachusetts after our Military Occupational Skill (MOS) training, but I felt it soonest with Louie. It enveloped me and I got the feeling that no matter what I'd ever do, I'd be welcomed and loved in his house.

He's religious, but more open-minded than I expected. He's firm, but loving. And, for a while, he took Rob into his home to live when Rob was an obnoxious, at-risk teenager playing around with drugs and alcohol. Fernanda thought he'd be safer under Louie's firm hand for a bit. So Louie is alright by me.

And when he steps in to handle some of the phone calls and family affairs, I am relieved. No one has to ask him, he just does it. Especially when I take the call from Rob's unit looking for him.

In a voice that doesn't sound like me, I explain that he died that morning and the caller is so incredulous she asks me to repeat myself three times. Fed up, I shout in the phone, "He's dead!" That's when Louie steps up to finish the call. I rock in my seat and stare at the floor. I hear Louie's voice but don't know what he is saying.

Lena asks about food, knowing of my pregnancy, and a dry bagel materializes. Gerry offers to take Aubrey home with her to be with the cousins.

"She's so little that I'm worried all the somberness and tears might be frightening for her. But whatever you think best. Whatever you want, Valerie."

At first I say no. I want her warm, *live* body close by because Rob's is so clearly not. But an hour or so later I change my mind. It will be better, healthier, for Aubrey to not be here – to go to Gerry's instead.

I wonder how much Aubrey knows about what's going on? She sits on the floor, chatting delightfully to her toys -- but that only makes it sadder somehow because now I see Rob lying on the floor with her last Christmas, building towers and houses with her fat new Legos while she watches them grow bigger and taller – a red one clutched in her hands. Every once in a while, she hands him a Lego.

And months after that, Rob on the floor again -- this time in his shirt and tie from work – answering Aubrey as she toddles about the room pointing to objects and asking, "This? ... This? ... This?" She wants to know the names of everything and Rob's proud smile that day will forever be with me.

I wonder if Aubrey will remember it.

After Aubrey and most of the family leaves, I make my way to the shower. I know with certainty that now, alone, I will be able to cry those real tears. They will come, I know.

Rob was my soulmate. *There's that* was *again*. We both knew it. Felt it. The day we met, we shared a pizza and conversation. The next week we started dating. Three months later we were married and exactly one year later, on our anniversary, our daughter was born. We were so closely linked in spirit we often thought the same thoughts, at the same time. Of course I will cry.

But alone in the dark, the real tears still do not come.

What am I going to do now? How am I going to live without you? I ask the wall. I feel no anger, only sorrow and emptiness. I feel as if I am perpetually holding my breath. *It doesn't matter how I live. I just have to. For Aubrey. For the new baby.*

Water pounds my skin and the shower mists blanket me, and even though I never pray any other time, here now in this shower I do. "Dear God, Whoever you are, please. Please give me strength and courage to make it through this day." I shudder to think what will follow 'this day'.

Dripping, I step over the side of the porcelain tub. Water soaks into the cotton bathmat. Reaching for a towel, I catch sight of a lone sunbeam shining through the slats of the blinds. It's a strong beam, bright and steady in the dark room.

Awed, I whisper, "Thank you, God. I know you're here." I dry off in silence and join the house of mourners with renewed strength. Still with heavy heart and full of sorrow, yes, but now with a quiet strength inside me. For the moment at least. But that's all I had asked for, strength and courage for the day.

CHAPTER 2

> "*I want to be with you every minute of every day just to see your beautiful smile and hear your sweet voice. You seem so perfect.*"
> ~Rob; love letter excerpt

Some of us are sitting in the parlor upstairs now. I sit in the computer chair near the dining room table. Also near the door. It seems we have a steady stream of callers and visitors. Friends, too. But mostly family. There's so many of them. I don't know how the phone tree started. Certainly I didn't call anyone. And I don't think Fernanda did either. She moans and weeps almost without stopping. It becomes all I hear.

Maybe Lena did it. Or Louie.

My boss sends a caterer with huge platters of food for everyone.

A reporter from a local newspaper comes, too. In a weird moment, I wonder if it's right to talk to him. Would it be tacky? Would it be an invasion of our privacy? Would I be sorry I did it later? Would he write a terrible article?

But I don't have the energy to deny the interview. And so it happens.

My friend, Stacey, and her husband come over, too. I am in the kitchen looking at the trays of food when she lets herself in.

"What are you doing here?" I am dismayed to see her up and around. She's on bed-rest for her at-risk pregnancy and I don't want her baby to die because she came to see *me*.

"Well, what do you think? I had to come." And she holds out her arms for me to hug. She is pale and stricken and I remember that she was Rob's friend first, before I'd even met her. Of course she'd come. She needs solace, too.

I rush to her and sink into her friendship.

"What am I going to do? What am I going to do? What am I going to do?" I say into her neck. I'm crying afresh and terrified.

And a Major from the Army comes by with condolences and a check. It's called a Death Gratuity. Morbid. Like a tip. For dying. Or for my pain and suffering for his death. A pay-off.

Actually it's to cover the cost of the funeral and I'm relieved to have it.

I slide my hands over the red countertops in Fernanda's kitchen. If people are here, they are blending in with the walls because I don't notice them. I only hear Fernanda crying. And shuffling. In her slippers. Her crying offends me. Not because *she* is crying, but because again *I* am not. A good wife would be howling in pain right now. A good wife would be trembling. A good wife would be sobbing. But I just stare. And so I'm bad. Undeserving. Maybe I deserved this – his death.

No.

I don't believe in a god that metes out punishment like this – or any other way actually. But still. This is pretty ironic when I think about it. Rob dies when Aubrey is almost two years old; Rob's *dad* died when Rob was three. Maybe this family is cursed.

Fernanda shuffles up to me.

"Ah, *Carida*," she says.

I blanch. *Sweetheart*. That was Rob's name for me. Not hers.

"I know exactly how you feel," she sobs. "This happen to me, too."

I look down and grip the countertop. She doesn't know how I feel. Yes, her husband died, too, but she wasn't pregnant; she had older kids; she had a stronger network of family; and she'd had *many* more years with her husband than I did.

"Maybe this family is cursed," I say out loud.

Fernanda looks like I've slapped her.

"Don't say that!" She whispers and yells it at the same time.

I look at her like a specimen under a microscope. Detached.

WE'RE STANDING IN THE ROOM WHERE FERNANDA SLEEPS. THE furniture in her own room is too big, towering over her, smothering, so she sleeps here. Fernanda and Lena stand opposite me across the twin bed. Like a face-off. I need to speak now or forever wonder if I should have.

"I just wanted to tell you." I start and stop, feeling my inferior twenty-six years, facing this matriarch. Her mouth is set with hardened grief. *How can a mother prepare to bury her only son?* I look down at the yellowish comforter.

"Uh. Rob and I just happened to talk about his wishes a couple months ago. You know, in case he died before me."

The irony.

Fernanda clutches the lapel of her blue housecoat with her left hand. Lena looks nauseous, her face paling while I falter with what I need to say next. My lips for Rob's voice.

"He said he wanted to be cremated." Fernanda muffles a squeak at my words and sways.

"He said he wanted to be cremated in the open air, without a box around him, because he didn't want to be trapped inside. Smothered. He wanted to be free. In the air."

My words stumble to a stop. I imagine her thoughts. *Her* son

... burnt to ash? I don't understand her visible revulsion, as if she's repulsed with my morals. Were Catholics not cremated? Maybe not.

At times like this, I have no patience for religion. Having been raised in a near-cult, I understandably steer clear of organized faiths. Yet the void I sense within me needs to be filled with something, so I occasionally attend Mass with Rob and Fernanda. It never seems to fit me though and I always feel hypocritical going.

Once Rob said I should start my own religion because I'd never find the one I was looking for. It didn't exist.

"Well." I shake my head. I certainly don't want to fight for a funeral pyre, something that isn't allowed here anyway – unless you lived on an Indian reservation. And she's so clearly horrified, I want to protect her from anything more traumatic. Though I wish I could honor Rob's memory, give him exactly what he had wanted. I wipe my nose with the back of my hand and look at the aged comforter again, then to Fernanda's eyes.

"It doesn't matter," I add. *But it did.* We weren't even married three years. Maybe I don't have a say in this. *But I should.* They knew him much longer than I did. But does that mean they suffer more grief than me? *No.* Do they have the right to decide what happens to him? Or do I? *Me. I was his wife.*

Oh, but she was his mother.

"We'll bury him," I say. "I'd like a gravesite to visit." And this much is true anyway. I feel a twinge of remorse. *Do my wishes mean more than Rob's?* Fernanda and Lena breathe collectively and one of them pats my arm.

I look through the doorway to the hall. I want Rob to have something from us in the coffin with him. But I can't think of anything that I can part with now. I want to hoard everything that he's ever touched, because what if I regret getting rid of anything? I decide on a picture. I like the idea of a picture with him, wherever he's going, like the ones in his wallet.

I find one from last Easter. In the photo we sat in our parlor – Rob, Aubrey and I – all ready for church services. We were in a green velour chair with brown wooden detail on the handles and legs. All of us shmooshed together. All dressed up. That's the one to send with him on his journey. That will remind him of home.

Fernanda, Gerry and Lena pack up a change of clothes for him in an overnight bag – as if this is somehow temporary. I give them the photo and leave instructions for the restoration artist to have it placed in Rob's breast pocket after he dresses the body.

Gerry pulls me aside.

"Do you think Rob should wear his Army Class A's?"

I laugh and cover my mouth at the unexpectedness.

"No. Just his black suit."

WHY DO WE DRESS UP THE BODY ANYWAY? SHOULDN'T THEY WEAR what they always do? It would be more real. More *them*. Rob shouldn't be in his Class A's, which he hated wearing. Or his black suit that he rarely wore. I don't even remember why we bought it in the first place. He should be in his flannel coat that he wore when he first saw the Pacific Ocean. And jeans. He always wore jeans. Unless it was Saturday, and he was on the computer. Then he'd be in his underwear. Boxers. I smile.

I don't think they'd go for that.

DURING EXODUS (OUR HOLIDAY BREAK FROM MOS JOB TRAINING), Rob and I had driven to Oregon from the Fitzsimmons Army Medical Center in Aurora, Colorado to visit my mom and dad.

On one of our day trips, my dad drove us to the coast so Rob could see the Pacific Ocean. He'd never been.

It was December and *cold*, but no snow. Just wind and rain. Rob took off his shirt and the quilted flannel coat my mom bought for him.

"What are you doing?" I pulled my black skullcap – Army issue – down over my ears and hunched my shoulders against the wind.

He took off his boots and socks.

I laughed with huge eyes. I looked back at my dad. He was whistling, hands in his pockets. He shrugged.

"What are you doing?" I ask again.

"Swimming." Rob flashed a smile and ran into the surf.

"You're crazy!" I yelled out to him. And then he dove in.

I whooped and jumped and laughed. He was crazy and I loved him.

My dad shook his head and grinned.

It's time to pick out his coffin.

Who wants to go?

It is discussed, surreally, like a trip to the mall.

It is decided that Fernanda and Louie will come with me.

First we sit with the funeral director at his shiny, yet subdued, desk. Places of mourning remind me of libraries with their quiet air of reverence. But shouldn't they be loud and chaotic, like an amusement park? It would allow for keening and pulling of hair and renting of garments. It seems a far healthier way to grieve to me.

We decide what days to have the wake, or viewing of the body, and that it's good to have two of them. People that work during the day can come to the wake in the evening to pay respects (another odd idea to me) and we'll have another one during the day.

It will be a lot of sitting and waiting and I figure I will do most of my crying there, so I arrange for Aubrey to be at my friend Maria's house during the wake. I don't want Aubrey to see me crying so much. And she loves Maria and Maria's son, Justin. Aubrey and Justin were born on the same day in the same hospital and Maria watched Aubrey while Rob and I were at work so I know she'll be happy and well looked after while I'm ... occupied.

The funeral director suggests a day for the funeral and I'm shocked at how soon it will be. Three days away. I blink.

"So soon?"

"Yes." He is calm and his eyes are tender. He doesn't explain why the need for expedience. My imagination starts rumbling and I tamp it down quick.

Now it's time to pick out the coffin. He pulls out a binder with pictures in sheet protectors and then we go to a room with fragments of coffins screwed into the wall. They remind me of specimens on a slide. Autopsies of organs.

"I don't know which to pick. There are so many," I say.

"What about this one?" Fernanda asks. The funeral director respectfully announces that it's made of titanium and has a seal around the lid so that no air can get in. It is guaranteed to preserve the body the longest out of all his caskets.

Fernanda touches it. It's baby blue and silver. I hate it. It's $20,000 and besides that, I don't want Rob's body hermetically sealed and preserved. I want him to biodegrade as fast as possible.

He wanted to be cremated, remember? He would suffocate in that, I think, and don't stop to correct my thought process.

I walk to the other side of the room. I like the idea of wood. I wonder what kind of wood he likes – *liked* -- best. I find a pretty cherry one, but it has religious figures on each corner. Mary holding a dead Jesus.

"I like this one but it seems a bit too religious for my taste. I don't know if Rob would've liked it," I say to Louie.

Already knowing that Rob wasn't the best of attenders for Sunday worship services, Louie asks, "Did he like going to church?" He clasps his hands behind his back, his blue eyes sad and in stark contrast to his white goatee.

Fernanda is right behind me -- the woman who would've become a nun when her own husband died, if she hadn't had any children. I don't want to say anything to hurt her, or betray Rob's memory. I'm not a tattletale.

I think for a moment. My eyes follow the glossy sheen on the casket and I look into the Mother Mary's anguished face.

"He loved the silence of the church. But when it was filled with people, he didn't feel God anymore. He felt Him more at the ocean." *The ocean was his church*, I think but don't say. Or maybe I do because Fernanda makes pained sounds over my shoulder.

I remember he told me once that his dream house would be situated so close to the ocean that he could come out in the morning before work with his coffee and watch the waves crash into the rocks. The water soothed him – watching it or being in it, it didn't matter.

Louie nods, like it makes sense to him and maybe he even feels that way himself. He nods like he knows Rob better that day, and maybe that gives him peace or maybe that hurts him even more.

"Then I think he'd like it," he says, still nodding. He moves a hand from behind him and points at the Mary/Jesus figure.

"That's *The Pieta*. It's a well-known work of art. It's subtle. Not like –" he looks around, " – maybe that." He points to a casket with a crucifix carved into it.

I decide on *The Pieta* casket. I feel reassured by her pain. She looks like me – like how I feel.

I don't know if I want to view Rob's body or not. Do I want to see a pale, grey version of the man I love? Will I feel drawn to kiss his stitched-closed lips and forever feel their coldness? Can I take that as my last memory of him?

As it turns out, I don't have to decide.

The funeral director has informed me that the "viewing" needs to be *closed casket*. I refuse staunchly to think about why – though I know it's because his blessed body, his lovely wonderful precious body, is mangled and the restoration artist can't do anything to fix him.

Fernanda is anxious. She flutters with her hands and walks

fast and gets more animated than I've seen her since the troopers came.

"*Nao!*"

She insists on seeing him. She refuses to put her son in the ground and not see him one last time.

"I'll go with you," Lena says. She is quiet and she holds her mom's elbow and they go back to call the funeral parlor again.

I'M IN A BLACK PANTS SUIT. I'VE BROUGHT FRAMED PICTURES OF ROB to put on easels and on top of the casket. We sit in chairs lined up on the right of the room. There are other chairs on the left where people can sit and pray or just be there. There is a guest book for people to sign just before they come in – like a wedding, but horrifically not. Over two hundred people come to "see" him.

The visitors file in and we, the most immediate family, are waiting to hug and hear their condolences. Another morbid parallel with weddings – the reception line.

I'm awed by all of Rob's friends and co-workers coming. People I'd never met, and some I didn't even know of. He'd touched so many people.

But the most surprising visitors are *my* co-workers. I break down when I see them all walk in together in a clump. I don't even know them very well. I didn't even think they liked me. And here they are. Because of me.

I watch as each visitor walks past and kneels on that prayer thingy in front of the casket – the one that's also in the churches amongst the pews for you to kneel on? They make the sign of the cross and clasp their hands together and bow their heads.

Every single one of them do it. Even the ones that aren't Portuguese – not that if you're Portuguese, you must also be Catholic. And I'm jealous. Jealous that they have something that brings them peace right now. Some deity that they rely on, and lean on, and *trust*. I don't have that. I felt hypocritical going to church with Rob, when we did go. And it's true I have a craving to fill that spiritual void I've carried for years and years, but God – with a capital "G" – just doesn't do it for me (despite the sunbeam in the bathroom that first day).

I am from a "witness-y" religion that had strange rules and expectations and yearnings for *something* more. To be better, to shine, to prove myself, to fill in the box, to be more than I could be – all for the sake of being "no part of this world," and following Jesus' example. Except that never made sense to me. Otherwise we would've been Jewish and had unconditional love for everyone, and I couldn't even befriend Jolene from seventh grade without getting in trouble with the elders in my congregation. She wasn't *one of us*.

After most of us in the reception line have gone up, and there are only a few stragglers coming in, I decide to go up, as well. I don't have any fancy hand gestures and I still don't trust the God I'd been raised with. But I go up and kneel, the vinyl cushion depressing beneath my knees. I lean against the railing and intertwine my fingers. I look at the casket and the rosary made out of yellow rosebuds draping across it.

I touch the casket with the four fingers on my right hand and say good-bye. I bow my head and cry and hold my breath so I won't make any noise and I say good-bye. I close my eyes and say good-bye.

Back at my seat, I panic. I flag down one of the funeral directors and ask him to find Rob's wedding ring. *What if it's already in the casket with him?* I have to have it. My last link.

Of course that isn't true. Aubrey's a piece of Rob, and my new baby – the one I found out about two days ago – it's a link. Or a gift, rather. Rob's last gift to me.

But the ring. I still have to have it.

The director nods and walks away. I assure myself that this is a good sign. He comes back five minutes later with a small Ziploc bag. In it are Rob's wallet and wedding ring. I'll look through the wallet later. I fish out the wedding ring and put it on my right thumb. I put the bag in my purse. I bend over my hands, which I've fisted together, and cry. And I say good-bye.

I WANT AUBREY TO GO TO THE FUNERAL WITH ME. I KNOW THEY'RE for the living – a ritual to say farewell. She needs to be there. Also, I don't want her to be sixteen years old and traumatized that she'd never been to her father's funeral.

My uncle is here, too. He's flown up from North Carolina for the funeral. My parents aren't though. My mom and I had decided that over the phone. She'd called back as promised once she'd gotten some air flight information.

"I can come now to the funeral, or I can wait until the following week," she'd said.

We debated the pros and cons. Or rather *she* did. She'd thought it all through so I wouldn't have to – leaving me with just the final decision. *I'll figure it out and call you back.*

"If I come now it'll be more expensive, but I'll do it in a heartbeat if you need me there. I'm here for you. Tell me what you want."

"Come after. We can talk more."

CHAPTER 3

> "God, I would give anything just to have you in my arms right now. I had your scent ingrained in my head all day today. No wonder I couldn't concentrate. If only we could spend every night together, life would be excellent."
>
> ~Rob; love letter excerpt

Rob was a spiritual man. He insisted that our daughter be baptized, he said the "Our Father" prayer when he was scared, but like I explained to Louie, he didn't like going to church.

When Rob did make it to Mass, he could sometimes pretend the people weren't there. He could close his eyes maybe, or pretend that the congregation's "And also with you" was merely his own voice ringing out, amplified.

But the organ? The organ ruined it. And the singing? Shit. That was the worst of all. How could he commune with his god when a nasally, warbley falsetto rang out from the balcony above him, accompanied by an ancient instrument that nobody played anymore except in a few churches? It was too much. He went when he felt extra obligated, but it was the ocean that connected him to his god.

So when the priest, Father Pawel, asks me about the service and whether there is to be singing, I assure him that "NO" we don't want it. I feel sure that Rob approves – wherever he is.

During the funeral mass, when the time comes for the organ to play ... the lights go out. *All* the electricity. The organ mutes, the microphones die.

My eyes widen and I hold my breath, a smile creeping across my face. *Rob.*

He did it. I know it.

Hi there. I'm still here. And fuck this organ. Love you all! Bye!

His final farewell. My shoulders relax a little and I squeeze Aubrey into a hug. Every time I think of this 'black out,' it will be like Rob is peeking around a corner, waving at me, and I will call it up when I'm feeling my blackest.

Louie goes up to the podium when the sound comes back on and he speaks. He cries and talks about taking Rob to McDonald's every week when he was little and watching him eat French fries with his pool of ketchup. And Louie says he is so glad that Rob is in heaven now because he lived a lot of hell on earth in his short time here.

I love Louie so much right now. To have been Rob's rock when he needed it, to have given him love and understanding when he was so low.

I wish I had thought to prepare something to say up there. Maybe I can ask him for his notes. I'd like to remember the things he said here today.

Father Pawel returns to the pulpit. I find irony that this priest, who is saying Rob's funeral mass now, was also the priest who married us six months ago. We got married in 1997 in Colorado in a gazebo across the street from the barracks, but we had a Catholic ceremony in 2000 in Massachusetts so his family could be present.

I look around at the people in the church, dotting the pews.

There's a man in Army Class A's and he's crying, but I don't know who he is.

And then it is time to carry the casket out. I had picked out Rob's closest friends and cousins to act as pallbearers. I like to think that they feel honored to do this for Rob and not horrified that I'd asked. TJ, Danny, Wally, Chris, Joe, Dave ... all file out the door and the rest of us follow.

We are to ride to the gravesite in a limousine. I sit in the back seat with two others, one on either side of me. The leather is a luscious cream -- the color of homemade vanilla ice cream. I stare at the back of the front seat thinking: *This would be where the driver's picture was, if this were a cab.*

My view through the windshield is the hearse in front of us. The back door hasn't been closed yet and the cherry wood of the casket blares out: *There's a body in here.* Rob's body. I know it isn't him in there. *He's* gone somewhere else, but the rest of him – the part he isn't using anymore – is in there.

My uncle from North Carolina slides into the front seat next to the chauffeur. His navy suit collar meets the skin below his graying red hair. His shoulders suggest that his hands lay in his lap without clenching and his head is bowed. And then he cries.

He gasps and sobs and his shoulders move up and down and I cringe. He is crying and I am not. He doesn't know the people in the limo, yet his vulnerability leaks out along with his tears. He didn't even *know* Rob – save the one time Aubrey, Rob and I visited him. I'm embarrassed for him.

But then I remember that I once went to a memorial service for a long time friend of Rob's. I cried, too. I didn't know anybody there and I'd never met the deceased. But I knew the people that loved her. I knew Rob and Chris and Susie and Stacey. And I knew that they were in pain and that hurt me, so I cried. My uncle's doing the same. He doesn't know anybody here except me, and he loves me and I'm hurting, and so he cries.

SMELL THE BLUE SKY

I HAVE A MILITARY FUNERAL FOR ROB. THE SOLDIERS IN CLASS A'S stand at attention and *Taps* plays, not by a bugler at the site, but on a black boom box placed conspicuously and irreverently on a nearby headstone. Tacky, but moving nonetheless. That's the part of the service I cry at.

At the end two soldiers in white gloves fold the flag with precision movements. One of them walks it up to me and places the flag in my upturned hands. He salutes me. Through my tears I am bewildered. Being an Army veteran myself, I know that soldiers don't salute other soldiers out of uniform. And civilians don't salute at all.

In fact, it was kind of a joke to the soldiers I buddied with when I was in the service. Whenever we saw civilians saluting to each other, on movies or something, we'd roll our eyes and shake our heads.

So I'm out of uniform, not a soldier anymore anyway, and I'm being saluted to. *What do I do?* I salute back. It seems the expected thing to do and it feels right. I always liked saluting -- showing someone respect and that you honored them – like taking your hat off when you entered a building. It just feels right.

AFTER THE SERVICES, WE GATHER AT OUR HOUSE. PEOPLE ARE THERE for hours. At one point I go outside to be alone a bit, like Lena did that one morning. After awhile I walk around the side of the house and come up past the open garage door. The garage is packed full of people with red-rimmed eyes telling stories and smoking. I make eye contact with a neighbor friend of ours – one who'd grown up with Rob and played in the forest and rode bikes with him – and Rob's cousin that owns a night club. I so want to be in there with them and to light up a Marlboro Red from a hard pack, but I'd quit smoking Thursday. The day Rob died.

I'm pregnant now. So I walk on past, lifting my chin at them. They nod in response, and one raises his cigarette, like his own version of a salute.

Rob and I used to smoke in the garage together. At one job I had, I worked until closing at the mall and I'd get home around ten at night and he'd be waiting for me. I'd pop my head in the door and say I was there and he'd get up from his computer game and come out to the garage and we'd sit for fifteen or twenty minutes and smoke and talk about our days. We'd talk about other things, too. The future, raising children, religion – and he'd make promises that I knew he would keep.

People trudge in and out until about nine in the evening and then we are left to the empty house. So empty without Rob. But people keep visiting in the days after. Ones that couldn't come to the funeral, or ones that know us the most and just don't want us to be alone. People bring food, too, and neither Fernanda, nor I, need to do any dishes for two weeks after Rob's death.

IT IS FINALS WEEK. I'D BEEN TAKING A SUMMER WRITING CLASS ALL this time, and now it's Monday night. Time to go to school. Should I go? I certainly have the mother of all excuses for skipping. What would Rob want me to do?

I don't want a whole term down the drain because I miss the final. I don't want to do it all over again, and frankly, I don't know when, or if, I will be going back to school now.

I go. I write my essay. I turn it in and let the instructor know that I won't be attending the very last class; he can mail me the results of my final.

"There's been a death in the family. My husband. I won't be here next week."

The professor looks old when I tell him. Like even his joy is creaky now. I feel bad for him. He doesn't know what to say. Neither do I. So I leave.

THE NEXT DAY AUBREY PLAYS NEAR ME AND I SIT ON THE GREEN couch. The slipcover is thin. I can feel the nubby texture of the original upholstery underneath. It feels as if I haven't left the room for weeks, but the funeral was just this past weekend. Bereavement cards scatter the desk's surface.

The TV is on to some placid children's show and Aubrey putters around her toys and books; her slippered two-year-old toes shuffle atop the waxed pine floor.

Careful not to trip over the area rug, she picks her foot up and holds onto the rocking chair's spindles for balance.

Draped across the rocking chair is Rob's BDU (battle dress uniform) shirt -- still starched. I'd pulled it from his duffle bag -- the one his National Guard unit sent with the Major that was handling the loose ends -- whenever it was that I got it.

These days I pretend that time doesn't exist anymore. That I have full control over it now. I can stop it and pretend my husband is still at Cape Cod doing his annual training for the Guard. I can rewind it to play over the last conversation I had with him. The one where I told him I was pregnant again. And put into slow motion his jumping up and down.

Sometimes I select scenes in the past of vacations we went on or words of love spoken in dark rooms; private jokes that sounded stupid to third parties.

I creak forward from the couch and pick up his camo'ed shirt -- swirls of green, brown and tan memories. I sniff it and put it on, lean back and pet the sleeves. *Am I touching him or he touching me?*

"Mommy." Aubrey's voice sharp contrast to Playhouse Disney. "That's Daddy's."

Did she think I was stealing it, as her Daddy was stolen from her? Did she think Rob would be mad at me for wearing his clothes? Was she just stating the facts as she knew them to be true? It was *'Daddy's'*. But not anymore.

"Would you like to wear it?"

I pull it off and hold it up to her. She toddles forward, chubby fingers grasping. I wrap it around her pink fuzziness, careful not to touch her two short pigtails lest she remember they are there and pull them out again.

Aubrey turns for appraisal and then crinkles her eyes.

"Mommy, a hug from Daddy!"

Indeed.

My throat constricts and I hold my breath so I won't cry.

I take her picture then; getting a hug from Daddy.

I'M CUTTING UP ONE OF ROB'S FLANNEL SHIRTS. GERRY WANTS A piece, and so do I, and so does one of Rob's friends. The shears snip and I sniff. I look for a fairly large swatch that isn't torn. Rob has worn this shirt to threads. It was his favorite. *There's that "was" again.*

Lena has followed me into our makeshift living room ("our" part of the house we share with Fernanda are the two bedrooms at the end of the hall; one as a bedroom, and one as a living room) and is now kneeling down in front of me. Watching me cut and make permanent something that Rob would rage at if he were alive. I almost smile. But it is too weighted down with the spongy thickness of my sadness and it does not emerge.

"Val, what does *cabre* mean?" She'd seen a note that Rob had left for me, signed 'Cabre.'

I frown at her.

"It's Portuguese. Don't you know?"

She shakes her head.

Now Gerry is coming down the hall towards us.

I address them both.

"Rob called me *Carida* and I wanted something to call him in return. Some special name. I asked him what "wolf" was in Portuguese, and he said *cabre*. So that's what I started calling him."

Now it's Lena's turn to frown.

"I thought wolf was *lobo*," she says to Gerry.

"I thought so." Gerry sounds uncertain.

Fernanda has now wandered over. I am still cutting.

"*Mae*, what does *cabre* mean?" one of the sisters asks.

Fernanda whispers words under her tongue, sorting them out. "Goat. Why?"

All three of us – Gerry, Lena and I – stop.

"Goat?" I ask.

And then I snicker.

And Lena does, too.

"What?" Fernanda asks.

"Rob told me that *cabre* meant 'wolf' all these years. That's what I've been calling him as a pet name for three years."

"Goat?" Fernanda says. She is taken aback for a second and then one single bark of laughter emits from her lips.

Just one. But it is all that it takes. We all start to howl with laughter. It tumbles over us and chokes out of us. Unwanted. Unbidden. But there, nonetheless, and we submit to it briefly.

Then we remember we are grieving and tuck away the laughter until next time. A more suitable time.

The day after my mom arrives for her visit, she walks into our living room with a gift. I'm on the couch and Aubrey's climbing in and out of her red and cream-colored Step Two toy box.

"Come here, Aubrey. I've got something for you," my mom says. She presents a charming baby doll to Aubrey.

"Oh!" Aubrey says. She smiles and hugs it to her. It's promptly christened "Gramma Baby."

During Aubrey's nap that day, my mom sits with me on the couch. It's our only piece of furniture in that room except for the rocking chair. The parlor, on the other hand, is hardly ever used. It's for special occasions and company. Mom is company, but to relax, we sit with the toy box and the comfy couch.

"Have you told Aubrey anything yet?"

"Not really. He was at A.T. (annual training), so he was away anyway. It's like he's still there actually. He isn't even supposed to be home yet. She probably isn't expecting him, but I need to tell her something. I don't want to just say he's dead. She wouldn't really know what that meant anyway.

"I don't want to say something terrible like, 'He's sleeping.' She'd keep waiting for him to wake up. Or *worse*, be afraid to go to sleep herself in case *she* died."

"And you don't want her thinking he'll be coming back any minute so you can't just say, 'He's not here,'" Mom says.

"And I don't want her thinking he's left because he was mad at us or didn't love us anymore. So I can't just say, 'He went away.'" I sigh. My head is hurting. I need food but I don't want to get up. I pick at a loose green thread from the couch cover.

"What if you say he *can't* come home? That would imply that he really would *want* to, if he could. But he can't. She wouldn't feel abandoned later. She would still feel loved. But she would know that he wasn't coming. She wouldn't be waiting."

I don't answer.

"Do you think that you need to find someone else right away?" Mom asks me later.

"No!" I'm surprised and vehement in my answer but not offended that she'd asked.

"It's just that in the past, you've seemed to need someone else telling you how great you were. You felt best when you were with someone else and being loved," she says.

"Well, yeah. But Rob changed that. I became whole with him. I don't need anyone else filling his place. I don't think that I'm supposed to be alone for the next sixty years, but I don't need someone right now," I say. I look in my lap and pick at my fingernails. It's true. I don't need anyone right now, yet I do know that there will be someone else someday.

While Mom is there, we sit at the dining room table and make lists and organize papers. She helps me call all our creditors and cancel credit cards and pay off stuff with the life insurance money that Rob had left us. She talks me through options I have for money market accounts and retirement accounts. We talk about me moving back to Oregon and whether I should continue with my schooling and what that would look like as a single mom.

A single mom? I think with a start. I haven't considered that yet. Single moms are girls that get knocked up, or are divorced. Not people like me. Not widowed.

Widowed? Another unfamiliar title. Widows are old and live in assisted living homes or creaky houses that smell of chewed up food. Or maybe they are middle-aged at the youngest; perhaps their husbands are dead from cancer or a heart attack out of nowhere. Not young like me.

I guess it's time to throw out the stereotypes.

Mom has to leave too soon, so we make plans for me to come to Oregon for a visit the following month. Aubrey and I will stay for three weeks.

ONE NIGHT AFTER MOM LEAVES, I'M LYING ON THE COUCH IN THE dark, watching television. Aubrey's asleep in her crib in the next room, the bedroom I alone share with her now. It seems I'm doing a lot of this TV-watching-in-the-dark thing lately, staying up way past when my head normally hits the pillow. It dulls the senses and for a second I can forget the worst of the pain. I figure it's better than drinking.

But mostly there is no forgetting. In the quiet times after Aubrey sleeps, I remember. I remember Rob's face after not shaving for a day or two. I remember when he'd stroke my hair and face. I remember that when we were dating and still living in the barracks at the base in Colorado, we'd walk in the nighttime and find places to sit and snuggle. Find private places where he'd get all shy, or he'd sing to me, or tell me his darkest secrets in Portuguese, so I couldn't understand them. I remember his laugh, and the chest hairs that would peep out from above his tee-shirt, and that when he got sleepy, he'd get extra snuggly. Or that when I walked away to do something, he'd pull me back to him for a kiss or a hug.

Sometimes he'd think of song lyrics just to sing to me, or play for me. It was like him reading me poetry.

The show is a re-run but I watch it anyway because I don't want to go to bed alone and know that he isn't down the hall playing his online computer game.

The phone rings. I need to pick it up because Fernanda isn't home from work yet – it's maybe only 9:30 in the evening. I don't want to talk to anyone, but I don't want the ringing to wake Aubrey. I lift my face from the arm of the couch.

"Hello?"

It's my Aunt Mary. Her husband is my uncle that came to the funeral.

"How are you doing?" she asks.

"I'm fine, I guess." I quietly clear my throat. It's been a couple hours since I spoke last.

I remember when my dad called me right after Rob died – a day or two later maybe. I was pacing the blackened parlor room where my happiness was stolen, the computer screen my only light in the sleeping house.

"You're strong," my father said.

"I don't feel strong."

And another phone call a couple days after that. Again, in the parlor. Why did I haunt this place? A place I rarely hung out in before Rob died. Was it because this was the last place I'd seen him alive? And therefore closer to him somehow, in this room?

This time the call was from my Uncle Phil.

It's a call I remembered long after all the other words of condolences were given to me. Long after the neighbor rang our bell and handed me a musical water globe with two doves in it "for your little girl" and a white business-sized envelope of cash collected for me from all the neighbors that I'd never met in the two years I lived in that house.

After a few beats of silence over the phone line I said,

"I don't know what to say."

It was honest. I actually didn't know the man, but he was one of my favorite uncles and the only family member, it seemed, that tried to keep in touch with me – save my mom and grandmother.

His answer was truthful, too. And poignantly perfect.

"Neither do I. But that doesn't matter. You won't remember what I say anyway. You'll just remember that I called."

My heart paused, swollen with love and relief.

So now it's his wife calling. Someone he married when I was a young teen and whom I know even less about. I think I'd met her twice.

"Are you praying?" she asks.

I close my eyes and quiet my sigh with effort. She's Catholic, too. It seems I'm surrounded in unwanted waves of Catholicism, every day holding myself apart a little from almost everyone I know. Not wanting to be preached to -- or converted -- in my weakened state, to a religion I felt was filled with frivolous hypocrisies. But at the same time desperately wanting connection and a warm soul to lean my aching head on.

"I'm trying." I give in and bow to the love and peace I know my aunt is trying to offer me. "It seems I've forgotten how to though."

It does seem ... relieving, to be able to spill your angst at the feet of a deity that claims to love you with no conditions – except the hundreds the priests throw at you.

"Have you tried praying to your husband?" she asks.

I'm silent.

"To Rob?" I ask, thinking I *must* have misunderstood.

"Yes."

As far as I know you can only pray to God, through Jesus' name. Anything else is, well –

"Isn't that blasphemous?"

Aunt Mary laughs. *Her uncle was a bishop, for Christ's sake!*

"No." I can hear the smile in her word. "If it helps, do it. It might lead you back into prayer to God. Get you used to praying again."

We say goodnight and I hang up the phone, thoughtful.

I turn off the TV and sit in the dark for a few moments.

"Rob? Can you hear me? I miss you."

CHAPTER 4

> "I can't wait to run my hands along your face and kiss your soft lips and feel your body against mine. You are truly one of the sweetest and kindest people I have ever met, and if you only knew how much that means to me, you might understand why I'm so attracted to you."
> ~Rob; love letter excerpt

About a week later, Aubrey toddles within eyesight. I'm sitting on the floor with my back against the couch.

"Mommy, where's Daddy?"

A shock wave from deep within Mother Earth's belly rolls and pitches my world – what's left of it anyway. I pull her to me and settle her in my lap. I stroke her brown straight hair and rock from side to side. She turns around and arches her back over my left knee. Her milk chocolate eyes bore into mine demanding an answer.

I knew this question was coming, and I *almost* had an answer for her. My mom and I decided it was vastly important that I answer this question correctly. We settled on he *can't* come home. He would if he could – because he loved us – but he just couldn't. He wasn't able to.

I know this in my head. I've practiced it with my mom, but now that Aubrey has actually *asked*, I'm paralyzed. I don't want to say it out loud to her. It would be too real. For, underneath, in the whispery shadows of my night-time dreams, I pretend that Rob is still at Annual Training.

I don't go so far as to tell myself that he'll be home "later," I just pretend he isn't home. I can go through all the motions of canceling credit cards, giving away his clothes and deciding if I should move back to Oregon to be near my parents, if I just tell myself that I am play-acting what I *would* do if Rob had died.

But here is Aubrey grasping at my fingers with her own sturdy digits, waiting for my answer. I sigh from the bottom of my diaphragm and squeeze her hands in love. I smile a brave mommy smile and pull out a picture book.

I can't bring myself to use the "D" word with her yet, so I open *No Matter What* by Debi Gliori – a book I bought Aubrey before Rob died – and begin to read.

The characters are two foxes. They have no gender and are only called Large and Small. *No Matter What* is a book about love, and how no matter what Small does or says or becomes, Large will always love Small. The book even goes into abstract ideas about mending love with smiles and kisses, but the best part – the part that hurdles us over "Where's Daddy?" is on the last three pages.

I read them out-loud to Aubrey again, for we have read this book many, many times.

> *But what about when you're far away?*
> *Does your love go too, or does it stay?*
> *Look up at the stars. They're far, far away.*
> *But their light reaches us at the end of each day.*
> *It's like that with love – we may be close,*
> *We may be far,*
> *But our love still surrounds us ...*

Wherever we are.

"DADDY'S LIKE THE STARS, AUBREY." I POINT TO THE STARS IN THE book. "He's far, far away and he can't come home, but he still loves us and we can feel it every day. He'll always love us – no matter what."

Blessedly she accepts this for the moment and her attention turns to something else. She slips out of my lap and wanders to her toys while I continue to stare at the last pages of the picture book. *Far, far away.*

I feel Rob's love surrounding me and know that *no matter what,* that will be true. Forever.

I sigh and close the book.

Later that night, and then every night for two weeks, when I lay Aubrey down in her crib I tell her I love her.

"And Daddy loves you, too," I say.

Her bright, shiny eyes widen and she gestures upward with her arms.

"He's far, far away!" she chants, and then she blows kisses in satisfaction.

It works. A little girl doesn't feel sad, and a mama can breath a little deeper into grief soaked lungs. *Thank you, Debi Gliori.*

WHEN I THINK OF ROB, MY THOUGHTS COME IN SNAPSHOTS. Montages of memories and inconsistencies. For instance, Rob was a quiet man, *and* a loud one. He said he was either loved by people *or* hated by them.

I wonder if anyone else knows that. Or did they know, for instance, that he slept with a rosary under his pillow but didn't like going to church. More lovely inconsistencies.

Maybe I should write these down.

I start cataloging everything I can remember of him and write down the snapshots in my journal. Like, he picked me flowers out of other people's yards. And he looked me straight in the eyes when we'd snuggle.

He loved the ocean and Adam Sandler. He played Dungeons and Dragons with his friends every Monday night and smoked pot but didn't bring any home for me; I never knew why not. He watched *Dharma and Greg* with me on Wednesdays but what he really wanted to do was play *Everquest* until 2:30 in the morning, and often did.

He slept in until noon on the weekends, which I hated, but did crazy things with me like make love in a parked car in a secluded unfinished subdivision or behind Army training hospital buildings, which I loved.

One time, before we'd gotten out of bed, he buried his face into my pregnant belly and said, "I can't wait to meet her." When we'd walk in crowded areas, he'd place one hand on my lower back and the other would curve around me, like a bubble, pushing and herding people out of the way; safe passage in a storm.

He had osteo-arthritis in his neck, knees, and ankles, and on the day when he crawled in the door at the end of his shift as a mason tender, he knew he needed a different job. He loved climbing about the scaffolding without a shirt on and swearing with his work buddies while he made cement for the masons to slop between bricks, but his body didn't. So he got a job at a hospital and fixed medical equipment. He didn't like having to put on a happy face and be nice to the nurses, so he only stayed there a year or so.

He had one foot that jutted out at an angle because it had been set wrong after a break. He also had a fake tooth.

He was incredibly prejudiced and I was horrified to discover that he thought stupid people should be killed so they couldn't make any other offspring. I wonder now if he had only been exaggerating.

Rob felt safe at the cemetery at night, and believed that the spirits actually kept him from physical harm. He said his father, who had died when Rob was three, looked out for him and saved his life multiple times – talked to him – but stopped suddenly during his adolescence. Rob always felt he'd disrespected him somehow, that he was then unworthy of the connection and it had dissolved. As a teenager he lived life recklessly. Drugs, alcohol, suicide attempts, depression, mental hospitals. He told me he always knew he was going to die young so he didn't worry about what he did with his body, but that that had changed when he met me.

It appears he was right after all.

He'd call me from work, when I was home with our baby, just to say 'hi' or called *me* while *I* was at work, and *he* was home with the baby, to say he missed me and loved me. We went on our "honeymoon" when I was 33 weeks pregnant, and had our first baby on our one-year anniversary.

The second will be born after his death, I think, and I touch my belly.

Rob said there was always a war going on inside him. The Good versus Evil. He was always on guard. He said he had to be prepared to murder the evil within him so it didn't take over and leak out. When he was mad, he'd put his head in the freezer to cool off.

He liked country music *and* heavy metal. More inconsistencies. But that's what made him so fascinating to me. I was never bored, always learning something new about him.

Our CD collection always amazed me. His favorite band was Rush, but he loved The Judd's, too. He'd find songs he wanted me to listen to and explain through them why they were important to him, like the director's commentary option on DVD's.

In Colorado, I'd wear his clothes when he snuck me off the army base to go on dates. He had the longest black lashes I'd ever seen, and a Boston accent. He said, "That's right!" with glee when I pronounced his name correctly the first time – *Pereira*. No one ever had. And I was the only one who called him Rob. Everyone else addressed him as "Bob," except his mother and grandmother, who still called him "Bobby."

He snuck cigarettes by walking around brazenly through the base. He said, "If you're trying to hide something, do it right out in the open. They never think to look there." His farts were always silent and when executed, he'd smile and say, "Don't breathe."

I stop my list making and look up from the couch. I wonder if I should really record this. Will the kids ever really want to know these things about him when they are older? *Of course*, I think, and write it all down. All that I can remember. It becomes like an obsession and I write faster.

He had a funny way of clearing his nose, like you'd clear your throat, by blowing air *out* his nose instead of in. It always sounded like he was laughing.

When he was in his teens, he lived with his Uncle Louie. He slept all day and would go out at night. He wore sunglasses a lot, and his canine teeth were oddly sharp, and because of that, for a while, Rob's little cousin thought that Rob was a vampire. He did nothing to dispel the myth.

In every picture I have of him with either Aubrey or myself by his side, he's smiling. Whenever he'd talk to his friend, Susie, on the phone his voice would melt into a different tone -- protective. I always knew when he was talking to her, and he called her on every one of her birthdays, no matter where he was in the world.

He bragged about how awesome I was to his co-workers, but when I'd shrivel into un-awesomeness and cry in his arms after a really hard day, he'd hold me and tell me he'd fix everything.

He'd take Aubrey and me on long drives through New England foliage, stopping only for Dunkin' Donuts coffee and cigarette breaks. He'd stare at ocean waves breaking into rocks along the beach and dream of a time when he'd be able to live close enough to see it every day. But he'd burn beehives with Raid and a lighter.

He loved logic puzzles and math and would find me in the

bathtub to tell me about a math problem he'd been working out in his head for days, even though I *really* needed the space from the world. But he also rubbed my feet after they'd swollen up at the end of a long pregnant day.

He was an enigma, a contradiction. He was absolutely devoted and loved me like crazy. I never doubted that. And after all these memories, I think that that is what I miss most about him. Knowing with every neuron and cell in my body that he was crazy about me.

What if I never find that again?

I tuck my journal away and check on Aubrey. She's downstairs with Fernanda and my little nieces – Gerry's daughters. Fernanda is feeding Aubrey in the high chair. Spaghetti. Spooning it into her mouth, even though Aubrey can do it herself.

I can tell Aubrey's not hungry because she is lolling about in the chair. She flops her arms about and looks at me sullenly as if irritated that I've allowed this force-feeding to happen.

I half-heartedly engage in the ever-going, ever-present meal debate with Fernanda. I think that because she's Portuguese, culturally she thinks people should eat much more than they are comfortably capable of.

"I think she's done. She keeps turning her head away. That means she doesn't want anymore."

"*Nao.* She hasn't finished her plate yet. Look." She shows me that Aubrey's only eaten a third of her helping, but I can tell by the spaghetti sauce smears that she'd loaded the whole plate to begin with. Aubrey wasn't even two. Of course she won't eat that. Sometimes *I* couldn't eat the plates Fernanda offered me.

I simply do not have the energy or spirit to carry on this age-old conversation. We live with Fernanda, she cares for us and takes care of Aubrey when I can't – which these days seems a lot. Fernanda buys our medications when we can't afford them, does our laundry, and prays for us. So I know we owe her, big time. But I don't feel comfortable with all she does for us anymore. It was one thing when Rob was here, but now I feel out of place without him as an anchor. A buffer.

Rob and I had been saving to make a move into our own apartment. After over two years of staying with her, we had wanted the privacy of sleeping naked, of her not knowing immediately if we'd gone to church that Sunday, and of raising Aubrey the exact way we wanted. I mean, we *do* raise her the way we want – or *I* do now – but there are plenty of things, in my opinion, that we were talked into in regards to Aubrey's upbringing and her immediate care.

Like the eating – how much and when – and whether she wears her shoes outside, or slippers in the basement. Fernanda doesn't like the way I clean up either. Often she comes behind me and re-cleans.

I'm sure she thinks she is doing a service and is only being helpful, but I'm sometimes irritated and territorial. I'll need to move us out soon. But where? I think I want to ultimately end up in Oregon near my family, so moving into an apartment at this point seems silly.

I kiss Aubrey on the top of her head.

"I'm going upstairs to lie down for awhile. I'm tired."

"That's alright," Fernanda says and scoops another bite to Aubrey's mouth. "We'll just eat and then the girls can play."

I walk upstairs, my feet defiantly bare against the carpet.

Why did he have to die? I don't believe that it was *his time*, or that God needed him in heaven, but maybe there's a reason why. I would feel better if there was a reason why. All my bones feel splintered, with sharp edges poking out, and each time I take a breath or move in any way, I hurt. I just want it to stop.

In bed I pull out my journal again. This time I'm going to write Rob a letter. My sister did this once when she was having trouble with her boyfriend. She wrote him all the things she wanted to tell him but was afraid to. Well, I'll write one today, too. For all the things I want to say to him, but can't.

Dear Rob,

Aubrey and I had a pretend birthday party yesterday at dinner. We wore birthday hats, used party plates for our food and Aubrey blew out a candle on a brownie all by herself. And then I remembered suddenly that you weren't going to walk into the door for dinner.

Aubrey wasn't going to light up with a gasp and a smile and a delighted "DADDY!" I wouldn't hear matching delight in your reply, "HIIII!" I wouldn't turn and smile at you and say, "Hi honey, how was your day?"

I found Colin Ray and Garth Brooks for the CD player and cried and cried. Aubrey was thankfully oblivious.

It helps that I remember you are still with me in moments of need like that. But I still cried.

I don't think I'm in shock anymore. I think I'm just sad now.

Aubrey moved into her own room last night. It's time for her to stop sharing a bedroom. She's two, so her being in the crib is making me nervous – she tries to climb out now. But even though she needs to be out of the crib for the baby's arrival, I still wish she could be with me.

She's my companion now. I already miss her sleeping near me. I can't hear her breathe on this monitor. It's too static-y. I guess I just don't feel so alone with her in my room. She seems so far away in your mom's old room. And there's the possibility that if she wakes in the middle of the night, she'll go to Fernanda and not me, because her bed's closer.

That would be intolerable. I would just break down and cry. I already feel like she relies on others too much for her care. It's like she expects others to care for her better and so automatically goes to them instead.

I don't feel like a good mother. I'm so distracted; I'm trying to carve out some space to be alone and center myself again, but I fear that it eats into Aubrey's time. I'm so tired every day now that I can't seem to find "my" time anywhere else. I basically go to sleep when she does and she wakes *me* in the morning.

Fernanda watches her and usually gives her breakfast in the morning while I shower because I don't have the energy to stay up at night and do it, or to set my alarm for five a.m. to do it before she awakens – sometimes she's awake then anyway! Then I have an aerobics class three times a week Fernanda watches her for. By the time I get home, lunch is already being prepared and Aubrey eats downstairs with her.

Lately paperwork and bills and phone calls keep me at the desk upstairs while Aubrey stays downstairs, and since my nieces come over every day and Aubrey wants to go see them, she stays downstairs until they leave in the evening.

I can't stay downstairs that whole time. I have things to do, things to clean or organize. So I go upstairs and leave her in Fernanda's care. I'm glad she has playmates but I feel as if I'm being less and less her mom. I try to console myself with, "I'm with her more than full-time working moms," and that I'm probably with her more than when I worked reception duties at the salon. (I quit. Did I tell you?)

I just feel insecure in this area without you to

tell me how great I am and how proud you are of me.

Please visit me in my dreams tonight and bring me peace. Tell me how proud you are. I really need to hear you say that I'm doing a great job right now – that I'm a great mom and Aubrey loves me, as do you. Please. I need this affirmation tonight.

My love to you. I hope you are doing well and having fun.

Kisses,
Valerie

p.s. Whenever Aubrey sees an American flag, she says, "Look! A flag for Daddy!" She's remembering when that soldier gave me one at your funeral.

I CLOSE MY JOURNAL AND PLACE IT ON MY BEDSIDE TABLE. I TUCK THE pen right up next to it so that they can touch, and I lie down. I hug Rob's pillow against my chest and smash my face into it. I cry without sound. Aubrey is still downstairs with Fernanda. Where else would she be? I cry because I'm lonely. I cry because I am alone. I cry because I'm a bad mother. I cry because Rob is dead. I cry because Fernanda is parenting my child instead of me.

And then I sleep.

CHAPTER 5

> "You're so beautiful, both inside and out, that it amazes me, and believe me when I say that I'll do whatever it takes to win and keep your love."
> ~Rob; love letter excerpt

It's November now, and I'm back home from my visit to my mother's. One morning I call the best man from our Colorado wedding and tell him the news. My heart is pounding in my chest and I feel like throwing up. Other than telling my mom an hour after I found out, I've never told someone close to us what happened. I hang up as fast as I can.

I know I can't feel the baby moving inside me yet, but I find myself thinking about it, wondering what and how to tell this little one about his or her father. It seems so surreal – this dying before the baby's born. I'm reminded of the sons and daughters of ship's captains lost at sea.

When I was pregnant with Aubrey I wrote her letters in my journal. I could do the same for this one. I listen for Aubrey napping in the other room. Nothing.

Good. Now where is that one journal? I look through a couple of drawers and find it under a stack of bereavement cards. I settle on the floor and riffle through the pages. A brochure is nestled amongst the pages and I pull it out, remembering that I snagged it off a bulletin board outside the YMCA many months ago. I frown. Maybe even a year ago. It promised a path away from stress through meditation. I read through it.

She's got a few different classes and lots of services she offers people ... and then all the way at the back, in small print, she offers a different service that I didn't expect. One that I didn't catch the first time I looked through the brochure either. She's a spirit medium. The brochure offers clients a space to contact their dead loves ones, and this woman even says she can contact our guardian angels.

I stop.

There are so many instances when I've felt Rob's presence in these past few months.

When I went to visit my mom in September, we went for a long drive. I was crying and feeling so terrible, missing Rob. We drove around a bend in the road and saw a beautiful, spectacular, day-glo-of-a-rainbow.

"Oh, how beautiful. I wish Rob could see it."

My mom answered, "Maybe he did."

Maybe he sent it to me. I wondered it for the rest of the day.

Or there was a dream once, which at the time scared me down to my toenails. So much so, that I went downstairs and insisted Fernanda come up and see if anyone was in the house. I had felt someone sit on the bed and when I woke up enough to sit up, I "saw" a shadowy figure run down the hall away from me. I decided later that it must have been Rob visiting me.

I'd had other dreams with him there just looking at me or holding me in silence. They were about nothing in particular – he was just visiting.

Is it really possible to connect with him now? Would it even work? Did I believe in life after death like this? What would Fernanda think of me if I did this? My cultish upbringing intoned that people who conversed with spirits would be consumed in a lake of fire. So, no give there.

I shake my head and snort. *But let me just say,* I explain in imaginary fashion – pretending all the people from my past are in the room with me, *I didn't reckon on being widowed at twenty-six years old.* Pregnant *and widowed … with a* two-year-old.

This is a lifetime's worth of tragedy. I figure I'll be granted immunity from the lake of fire on this one. Even though I'd left the "church" years before, I still find myself reacting in knee-jerk fashion to topics that had once been taboo before – blood donation, spirituality, philosophy, life after death – and it irritates me. I flick the brochure onto the floor and stare at it.

And it isn't like I would be jumping at this head-first. I tried going to a grief support group for young widows a couple of times – but it was lame. I guess I wasn't ready to speak in such a large group. After all, it's only been three months since he died. The folks in the group all seemed to be past my stage of grieving and I always left feeling defensive or stupid for crying. Not the kind of healing place I was looking for.

This wouldn't be mainstream, of course. I inch forward to the brochure and look up her phone number. My lips squish together and I sigh. *There's no way I feel comfortable calling her.* I scan further down the page. *Maybe there's an email address.*

My hands tremble at what I'm about to do. I gulp a huge section of air and push it out. My consciousness cracks open a teeny bit wider. If this brings me peace, then so be it. I take the brochure to the computer and promptly, before my nerve leaves me, compose an email to Sandy. Sandy, who calls herself a soul coach.

Lake of fire, here I come.

I hit send and then immediately start worrying that I shouldn't have.

CHAPTER 6

> *"Dear God, Take care of Daddy. Amen."*
> ~a prayer from Aubrey at two years old.

I'm lonely and sad, and especially so for Aubrey and the new baby. Imagine having your father die before you are born. I pull the sleeves of my sweater down over my hands and squeeze my knees to my chest – huddling on the couch.

Rob should be here see the new baby christened, take them to ice skating lessons and Little League games. Read them stories and play with them. Sing to them and cuddle them – or to *me*. Be here to watch Aubrey graduate and get married. We should be raising the huge family we wanted, buying a house together and getting a dog.

I want him here to share stories with – to live and grow old with. To laugh with. *Will I ever really laugh again?* What happens if I meet someone new? How could I look at myself in the mirror and not see a traitor? How could I remove our wedding pictures off the walls or take off my wedding ring without hating myself? How could I have sex with another man and not feel guilty and hideous? How could I settle for anyone less than my soulmate?

I've known loss before. Rob wasn't my first partner. After my divorce to my first husband, I was bitter and hard and angry. I didn't want to be a girl anymore because it made me more vulnerable. I didn't even allow people to call me Valerie. It was *Val*. That seemed harder somehow. An armor to wear. I joined the army and learned how to shoot a gun. I told raunchy jokes with the soldiers I was stationed with, and wore aviator sunglasses like Tom Cruise in *Top Gun*. I was tough.

And then I met Rob. Rob liked soft. He liked girlie. He liked me. Even when at my worst. When we first started dating, I put my snarkiest foot forward just to see if he would take it. And he did. He could take me. Anyway I showed up. Girlie, or not. Tough, or not. And we just fit together. It was great.

But another? How could I ever find *another* man that cracks my spirit open and dances in my uniqueness? What if it's not possible? What if I never find someone?

I'M LATE GETTING TO THE SOUL COACH'S THIS FIRST SESSION. I've remembered the time wrong. Sandy is petite with dark hair. She smiles big with white teeth and exudes comfort. I don't realize how nervous I've been about meeting her until I see how normal she looks. She offers me tea and I use the bathroom. It's decorated with a brightly colored fish shower curtain. Blues and yellows.

My session is in her sunroom. Pastel cushions on white wicker, a small fountain splashing and serene music wash over me. I settle into a chair across from her and put my feet up. The mug in my hands holds tea still too hot to drink.

Sandy closes her eyes and rests her hands, palms up, in her lap. Her legs are uncrossed.

In the silence I wait for messages from Rob. She begins by describing him and who he's with. Someone named Reginald, and another man that strikes me as Rob's father – though I don't know why. And I don't know anyone by the name of Reginald. *Hmm.*

I'm here with an open mind, I remind myself.

"Don't be fearful. I don't look like that anymore. Don't remember me

like that," Sandy says. This is obviously Rob talking through her, but her voice doesn't change. Her face doesn't contort; she looks peaceful and for a brief moment I envy her. I envy her peace and seeming ability to talk to Rob. *I* want those things.

I lean forward, greedy for more words from him. While I wait, I go over what he just "said." I take this to be a message for Fernanda and Lena. They were the only ones to see his body in the coffin. But I accept this message for myself, too. I have my own slideshow of possibilities scrolling through my mind. My images are probably much worse than what Fernanda or Lena saw in the coffin that day.

For the next two hours I listen to Rob's messages and ask a few clarifying questions. It's a strange three-way conversation that I suspect I'll never forget.

"Make your decisions out of love for the children."

"Don't worry about finances. There are some – plenty – coming your way. You just don't see it yet."

I've come here wanting to believe that this woman could really contact Rob. I mean, who wouldn't? The opportunity to talk to a loved one that has passed? *Duh.* But so far I haven't heard her say anything that any carnival fortune-teller wouldn't have.

I've only come with one question for Rob.

"Did you choose to die?"

My hands are closed in fists around themselves and my shoulders are hunched, waiting for the answer.

He responds with Sandy's help.

"Not like you think. Soften the word death. It's more like a doorway. My awareness had an agreement."

I wipe the tears away as I sob and nod my head. Of course. It would be that way. The way that he said.

"Rob's telling me that you are not to blame yourself for him dying," Sandy says. "It was part of the contract. *'We'd decided it before we were even born,'* he's saying."

She pauses again and closes her eyes.

"He says he has instructions for you," Sandy says.

"Okay." I sit up straighter and wonder if I should write this down.

"One was coming to see me." She pauses, listening, then laughs.

"What?" I ask.

"He's saying: *She's stubborn, isn't she?*"

I smile through my tears.

"He says the stubborn part was for '... *letting go. Not letting me go. In fact, I'm not asking that — just letting go of your belief system.*"

Then she says for him: "*Once you allow the fullness of my presence into your heart, your spirit will find peace — you'll be at peace.*

"*Remember the promise we made three years ago. Ignore the 'until death do us part' part. We do not part with death. You didn't marry me for my physical body, you married my spirit. The part that defined me. Who I was. That part will never die or leave,*" Rob says.

I'm not alone. That's what he's telling me. I'll never be alone. He'll always be there whenever I need him.

"What are you doing there, Rob?" I ask.

"*Getting my feet wet. I'm still getting used to not having a body. I can get really small and then really big. It's cool,*" Rob says.

"He's kissing your belly." Sandy smiles. "He says the baby will look like you."

"Can he hear my thoughts?" I ask Sandy. She answers for him.

"*I don't invade your thoughts but if you direct them to me I'll "hear" them,*" Rob said. "*Do you hear me?*"

"No. I wish I did," I say.

"Don't worry. You will," Sandy promises.

"Did you do what you needed to in this life? Or at least some of it?" I ask.

"*I met you. And the kids.*"

I swallow and look down at my lap. I shake my head. Was that enough? Were we enough? How could *I* be enough? I pay Sandy and leave, but I've made an appointment to see her again. I'm coming back. She's impressed me.

I FEEL OVERWHELMED WITH DECISIONS TO MAKE AND ERRANDS TO RUN and legal matters to attend to. I'm so tired all the time and I want to find some inner-peace and strength. I know it's there somewhere. I just don't know how to find it.

Writing would help, but I don't seem to find the time or energy, nor the creativity to do it. It all seems to be lacking. I hate feeling sorry for myself; it's wimpy and non-productive.

I'm fighting my initial response to "Let's hurry this up and get it done so I can move on to the next thing." That doesn't work well with grief. I know from personal experience.

When my first husband left me, my response was: "Well, crying's not going to bring him back, so, let's get on with it." Three months later I suffered panic attacks, took medical leave of absence from work, took medication, moved a couple times, developed some unsavory habits and became bitter and unhappy. In the Native American tradition, I named myself *Screaming Tree*.

I don't want all that to happen again. It can't. I have a two-year-old and a pregnancy to handle.

If I knew I'd see Rob again in another life, I think I could bear this pain now.

I start reading up on reincarnation.

GRIEF SUCKS. MY WORLD HAS BEEN TURNED INSIDE OUT WITH THE tags and seams all showing. It's messy and weird and I just want to sleep and hope it all goes away.

I've heard that some people think the nights are the worst, but I don't. At night I crash asleep with the weight of stagnant grief saturating me and holding me down. The *days* are what scare me with their hollow hopelessness. If I'd hit my head and suffered a concussion, I wouldn't feel any different than I do now. Hazy, confused, frozen, slow, nauseous.

I don't know what to do with myself.

I don't know how to be anymore.

And that's a big deal to someone grieving. I don't think others know that. Grieving people are paralyzed with uncertainty. And least I am. *Who am I now?* Because I'm not the same as before Rob died. I *was* a wife, but not anymore. I *was* part of a couple ... with couple friends doing couple things. Now I'm not.

How do I re-define myself? How do I become a new person? And do I even want to? My breath stills. I don't think I want to. But I don't have a choice, do I? My labels have been stripped from me when I wasn't looking – naked before my friends and family, I am no longer who I used to be.

I'm a single mom now, but I don't know how to be that.

When I met Rob I hated country music and loved 80's pop, classic 70's rock and that alternative pop that came out in the 90's, like, *Cranberries, Goo Goo Dolls* and *Better Than Ezra*. Rob introduced me to bands I'd never heard of, like *Rush*, and plagued me with Garth Brooks, John Michael Montgomery, *The Judd's* and Clay Walker until I loved them.

Now that he's dead, I still listen to them, but something strange is happening. I've started listening to music I haven't heard in years: *Erasure, OMD, Dishwalla* and *The Steve Miller Band*. This is curious to me.

It wasn't like Rob didn't allow me to listen to music I liked, but rather I adapted to the music he listened to and shared it with him. I enjoyed it. But without him to share it with, I start *remembering* what I used to listen to – in a way, re-establishing myself as an individual. Not a couple. I'm going back to my *single* music.

Remembering who I was before I met Rob (and still am now) seems like a good idea. Grounding.

It's empowering to reinvent myself though. It may even be somewhat of a relief to start from scratch. Tiring, yes. But a chance to shed the parts about me I don't like. And when I emerge from this terrifying trek through the bowels of my fear, sadness and loneliness, I can be proud of my growth and strength.

At least, that's what I tell myself on the not-so-bad days.

The funny thing is, I can't just go back to being single – though that's what it looks like to the rest of the world. I don't get to go back to the way things used to be before I met Rob. But I have to start somewhere, and so this is what I do:

I get up every morning, love my daughter, try to connect to the Universal Source (my new word for God), talk to Rob on paper and in my dreams, grow a baby inside me and listen to my heart. I breathe in and out, and learn how to be a single mom and not a wife. I take Aubrey to her friends' birthday parties where people take pictures and I'm not smiling in them. I go to W.I.C. appointments where the case workers tell me to eat more and I cry in the car on the way to swim classes and stop to get Dunkin' Donuts coffee and bagels on the way home. I journal and I meditate. I put one foot in front of another and breathe in and out.

ONE MORNING BEFORE CHRISTMAS, MY FIRST WITHOUT ROB, I PULL out my journal. I've been feeling so negative lately that I want to capture something positive and I'm feeling good today.

> Dear God,
> Thank you for the beauty of a candle. Thank you for the smell of pinecones and cinnamon and cocoa. Thank you for the company of my two-year-old beautiful daughter. Thank you for the life growing inside me. Thank you for the lessons I'm learning every day. Amen.

I AM READING A LOT THESE DAYS. IMMERSING MYSELF IN A BOOK IS not something new and my friend, Maria – knowing my interests – bought me one that I'm diving into. It is so what I need to hear right now. It's called "The Destiny of Souls" and talks about reincarnation in a way that my skeptical brain admires.

A doctor of psychology was practicing hypnosis on a patient one day, regressing him back to early childhood in an attempt to heal some past trauma and the patient regressed back to before he was born. This had never happened to him before so, with his analytical scientific brain, he started interviewing patients under hypnosis and regressing them back to this in-between time and questioned them. This book was a compilation of the case studies.

I, who had never even once considered reincarnation before Rob died – indeed was taught expressly against it in my church – am slowly becoming a believer. A series of maybes flit through my waking hours. Maybe it's only because I want so much for this concept to be true. Maybe talking to spirits of loved ones and guardian angels is all make believe. Maybe I'm just making it up as I go along. I ask Sandy about this in one of our weekly sessions.

"So what. Maybe you are. If it brings you peace, who cares?" She pauses then and smiles. "But maybe it is true. Maybe you really are talking to them. That's what I believe is happening," Sandy says.

The books I'm drawn to help build my new identity. It becomes a platform to stand on. Maybe it's boring to others, or in their "freak-out" category. But I don't care. I am fascinated by this topic and feel myself coming slowly alive again while contemplating it. Reincarnation feels soothing to me because then I know I will see Rob again, and the crushing weight of grief shifts a little.

I'm embarrassed to admit that angels have started inching their way into my psyche, as well. Perhaps this is due to the Catholic family I'm surrounded with, but all of a sudden I don't seem to mind the idea of them anymore.

Having a guardian angel assigned to me means I will never ever in my entire life be alone. My skin can breathe a little deeper. And if I reincarnate over and over again, surely I reincarnate with the same souls. Some of them anyway. Rob, for sure. So now I have a constant, forever family. I am loved, I am not alone and I have spirits (and people) that have my back.

I want Aubrey and my other child to have this same serenity I've discovered. But the concepts I've recently learned are not easy to explain to little ones. How can I teach them to be spiritual? Is prayer enough?

After months of sessions with Sandy, I decide to pair her automatic writing with my aunt's suggestion of praying to Rob. I think automatic writing is a dumb name for it. Sandy explained that you write a question at the top of the page of your journal and then sit quietly with no distractions and listen for the answer. She assured me it would be weird for a while, but that if I just had some faith and believed in the process, I would start getting answers. Sometimes the answers wouldn't make sense, but she promised that if I went ahead and wrote them down, I'd most likely understand it later.

Aubrey was down for a nap, so I sat in the rocking chair in the next room over and wrote my question at the top of my journal page.

"Rob, how shall I teach our children to worship and meditate? Please guide me so that Aubrey and the new baby gain peace and spirituality for their highest good. What steps should I take?"

I hold the pen loosely in my hand and scratch my nose. I need to be relaxed and open. I can't second guess myself. Just be here now and write down everything I think, hear or imagine. I'll sort it all out later. I sigh and lean back in the rocking chair and close my eyes. I let my mind wander, but still keep my question at hand, in the back, resting.

And then ...

Trust in your heart.

My breath catches. I stop rocking in the chair and open my eyes. I hurriedly write it down. I ponder for a few seconds about the voice. It wasn't so much that I heard it, it was more like I sensed the words. They just appeared in my mind.

My turn. I put pen to paper again.

"I need more direction than that," I write. Again, I close my eyes and listen.

It's not my place.

What?! I furiously scribble my next thought: "You are her father!" I snap my eyes shut with a strange mixture of excitement in this conversation (*I'm talking to Rob!*) and anger that he's being so nonchalant about this.

Not the father of her soul.

Tears spring to my eyes and I hold my sob in. I keep writing.

"Well, then, as much as it pains me to admit this: I am not the mother of her soul either. But she still needs direction and I'm not comfortable with a Catholic upbringing. Please help me find a positive, caring and spiritual way to teach Aubrey and the new baby to worship and feel spiritual peace."

Again, the answer comes so fast I am amazed. Is this really happening? Am I just making this up?

Teach her to find herself, as you are doing. Be patient. You won't have all the answers at once. They'll come to you in the moment. Once you stop listening to others (conflicting) you'll be able to hear yourself and you'll know what to do.

I trust you and believe in you. You are wonderful. I hear you tell Aubrey that, and it is perfect. That's what you should do. Believe in yourself. Love yourself, even when it feels like no one else does.

There are many who love you, even those on Earth. You are not alone. I am with you, your guides are with you, and others from our soul family. Trust in them. They will not fail you. You will not fail yourself.

I know you miss me. In a way I miss you too, but you are *with me here, so I know it is not the same for you as me. I'm sorry you feel pain, but you are strong. You will get through this; you will find happiness.*

I saw, like in a movie, Rob putting his hands on my head.

Don't ask yourself so many questions. You will know the answers when you get the question at hand.

I continue writing. "There are many things I miss about us being together. I know that I'll see you again and that my grief doesn't need be as intense as if I believed you were gone forever. But there are still things I grieve about you not being here now.

"Like not sharing pictures of Aubrey with you, or milestones she reaches, how well she talks, or how she'd light up when you were around. I know you can see these things taking place, but I still miss the sharing of them. I miss cooking your dinner, talking in the bathroom until four in the morning, going for drives, all three of us playing on the floor, going on trips with you, talking about things that were important to us, sitting in the garage smoking cigarettes.

"I miss *being* with you. I miss the companionship. I realize the probability of meeting someone to finish sharing my life with, but I don't want to settle on a man that doesn't meet my standards because I want companionship."

I see, in my mind, Rob shake his head.

That won't happen. I won't let it happen. You won't let it happen. You are stronger than you think. You'll stand up to your beliefs and value system and, in your soul, you'll know if it is the right thing to do.

"I know that there will never be another soulmate – another you – so in a sense, wouldn't I be settling anyway?"

He sighs with patience, like I am a little child.

You will know what to do when the time comes. Stay here in the now. You'll do fine. Believe in yourself.

I am crying.

"Thank you so much for your encouragement. I love you and miss you."

Rob drifts away and smiles and blows me a kiss of wisdom and confidence.

I hear Aubrey start to stir in the next room. I look at what I'd last written, then turn my attention back to the spirit realm, but I don't get anything. Aubrey's louder now and the moment is gone. I set the journal aside and wipe my tears. I go to the bathroom and blow my nose, and then go to Aubrey and change her diaper.

God still feels a little distant to me, but the angels and teachers in the spirit realm bridge that gap and someday, if I need to, I can connect with Him. But right now Rob will do just fine. That's all I need. Him and Sandy. Sandy is my guide.

My days with Sandy are a blessing. I look forward to our visits and the peace I feel after working through my fears and sadness and guilt with her. Yet that feeling of acceptance and rightness with my place in the universe last only a couple days before the aching descends again.

I share this with Sandy one day and she recommends guided meditation. She has a CD that will help. And it does. It starts to extend my peace of mind little bits at a time and I find that after a few weeks, I can make it to my sessions week to week without too much pain. It appears I'm healing.

WE'RE IN THE DOWNSTAIRS KITCHEN, FERNANDA AND I. THE ONE with the red countertops. We're eating a meal together. Just a quick lunch. Aubrey's already been fed and she and her little girl cousins are all playing with toys that Fernanda saved from Gerry, Lena and Rob's childhood. Disney channel is on in the background.

"I put our rings on a gold chain," I say. I hold it out from my neck to show her. Gold chain, gold rings. Only my engagement ring adds a bit of color and sparkle. Tiny emeralds around a bit of diamond.

"My hands are swelling a bit from the pregnancy and I don't want them to get stuck. I read somewhere that a woman went to bed just fine and by morning her hands were so swollen, they had to cut her rings off her hand." I shook my head and dropped the chain. The rings did a little thud against my breastbone when they fell back down to my shirt. I fill my fork with another bite of pasta and broccoli. My eyes drift to Fernanda's hand. Decades after Jose died, Fernanda still has her wedding ring on.

To be honest, I think I'm using the "retaining water" bit as an excuse. Rob's been dead six months. I'm working through some grief and sadness and guilt with Sandy and I'm feeling a need to move on a bit. Not a forgetting, of course! Just – moving forward a ways. After all, I'm still actually wearing them. Just not on my hand.

I want to know that I'm getting better. That I'm crawling out of my hole. And for some reason, moving our wedding rings from my hand to my neck seems to feel like forward momentum.

Fernanda sees me looking at her ring.

"Everyone's different," she says.

I look down to my food and close my eyes. The better to hide them rolling. I

breathe a sigh.

"I know. I know you haven't taken yours off. It's just that – I don't want anything to happen to them. I can put them on after the baby is born and my hands stop swelling."

This is true, but feels made up to me all the same. I drop the subject and we finish our lunch in silence.

CHAPTER 7

> "I've been thinking about you all day. It doesn't matter too much to me what we do tomorrow. As long as we can be together all day, I'll have a good time."
> ~Rob; love letter excerpt

One winter afternoon, I find myself at Stacey's house. She is still pregnant, though has lost one of the twins inside her. Our little children are playing and we are both in the kitchen. Before Rob died, we talked every day on the phone and I visited her at least once a week, but lately this is no longer true. I read and do water aerobics because my back hurts a lot during this pregnancy. I write almost constantly in my journal these days. It seems to be the only thing that helps me make sense of the swirling madness in my brain. I also seem to be spending more time with Maria.

This is quite natural, I tell myself. Maria watches Aubrey while I go and see Sandy. I've told no one else about my sessions. They are so far from Catholicism, that they're off the radar. Yes, they know about them in that I'm going to them, but I only identify them as counseling sessions, which is *so* true that I don't even blink saying it. And Maria is equally fascinated with guardian angels and spirit guides. She picks my brain after every session. I tell her about the visualization techniques that help me to rid myself of my guilt and fear, and I share anything I learn about how to contact our guides. *That* she seems especially interested in.

So this winter day that I'm with Stacey, I decide to open up a little about my Sandy sessions. I feel an alteration in the closeness of our friendship, and I want to re-connect with her.

"I'm feeling such peace from my time with her, Stacey," I say.

Stacey wipes her hands on a towel at the kitchen sink and walks to her mantle. She lights three candles.

"One for Baby, one for Beth and one for Bob," she explains. Baby means the twin inside of her she knows she's already lost, Beth was her sister-in-law that had died only months before, and Bob – that was what she called Rob. Everyone did, in fact, except me.

"Have you ever thought about contacting Rob or Beth?" I ask. Her eyes are round as she shakes her head.

"It's helped me so much – I can understand the why a bit more and that's made all the difference for me." I wait for acknowledgment or a request for more information. This is so fascinating to me right now – literally a whole new world. And one where I can stay connected to the man I love.

I can feel Stacey's despair and sadness whenever I visit her. I want my friend to feel the same peace that is starting to sink into my frozen organs.

I offer to pay for a session. Maybe if she or her husband go and at least *meet* Sandy, they can find some similar comfort.

"No, thanks," she says. And that is pretty much it. She doesn't want to talk about it anymore. I feel a shriveling up inside me and I fear that our friendship might not sustain this. I'm not angry, nor do I see this as a rejection from her. I love her. She's my best friend. But it is obvious to me now that Stacey and I are in different places on our healing paths. She has to find her own system to ease her pain; mine doesn't fit her.

I leave her apartment that day with sadness and resignation.

I try to be real careful about who I tell my new beliefs to so I don't create any discomfort. And truthfully, because it's less than mainstream, I'm worried that I'll be rejected or ostracized. So, at this point, Maria seems to be the only friend that accepts all of me. Maybe that's not fair, because I'm not sharing all of me with others, so how do I really know if other friends or my family would accept the all of me? But right now I just don't have the strength to try out that hypothesis. And so I continue visiting Maria and she and I get closer.

I could say that Maria's a willing listener when I most need one, and Stacey doesn't want to hear about it because it makes her uncomfortable. But mostly what I think is, that the speed at which I'm moving through my grief is different from Stacey's speed. I want to move ahead, away from the negativity that poisons my urges to get up and move forward through the pain and fear.

Or maybe she's just grieving in a different way than I am – which is pretty much a guarantee when it comes to grieving – and I need to go on my own journey, necessitating that I leave her behind. Not because I want to, but because she can't follow me. Knowing that I don't need to be alone during this process is reassuring and helps me make that next step. But I still feel guilty doing it.

Stacey was with me through so much and welcomed me into her life when I first moved here, friendless. And now I'm turning my back on her? I feel evil and old and hollow and mean.

And I also feel like surviving. Climbing out of this hole just might mean spending more time with Maria right now. *Sigh.* (It seems that sighing is all I'm doing lately.)

I BEGIN FEELING BETTER AND BETTER BETWEEN SANDY SESSIONS. Stronger. More capable. And I'm excited about my progress in communication with my guides. I feel hopeful checking in with them everyday. And I feel like I'm fulfilling something. As if I'm finding that inner-self again.

I've asked Sandy and my guides about doing a past-life regression and keep getting a 'you're not ready' answer. However, I'm still plagued by my fearful panicky thoughts – thoughts I've had since I was *thirteen*. They're always violent. Something terrible happening to me or to my loved ones – car jackings, kidnappings, death, you name it. I think regression would be helpful in determining where my fears stem from and possibly reaffirming my thoughts on why Rob died. I think finding these things out would cause forward momentum in my growth, but I get the feeling that Sandy thinks discussing other issues would be more in line with my highest good. I resolve to ask her.

AT MY SESSION THE NEXT DAY, I LEAN FORWARD IN MY CHAIR watching Sandy. She is using a pendulum at the end of a chain to douse for my answer. She asks the angels and guides if it is the right time for me and the medal swings around.

"What does it do when the answer is 'no'," I ask.

"It doesn't move."

So my answer is yes, and with a mix of excitement and disbelief warring in my mind, I sit back in my chair and close my eyes.

CHAPTER 8

> "I can't wait to take you back to Boston with me and show you the town and show you off to my friends and family."
>
> ~Rob; love letter excerpt

In order to get me super relaxed during sessions, Sandy often walks me through a guided meditation. Sometimes she takes me climbing up a mountain path where I find a wooden cabin in as close to paradise as I can imagine. I climb and climb, spiraling around the circumference until I reach the summit where the cabin is. Then I'll walk through a door in the cabin that takes me down a long staircase. Or she might take me to a classroom with a blackboard where I am to write the alphabet one letter at a time, and then erase the one letter before writing the other. Or sometimes she might have me count backwards.

I'm still fully conscious of everything in the room and I know I can open my eyes whenever I want to. I just feel uber-relaxed. Like the state where you are almost asleep, but not.

"What do you see?" Sandy asks today.

I look through the black behind my eyes.

"I see a young woman with chestnut hair."

"What's she doing?"

I can hear the tabletop water fountain behind my chair.

"She's meeting someone through blue mists," I say.

"Who is it? Do you know?"

"Um … I feel like it's Rob, but it doesn't look like him. He's got blond hair and blue-ish eyes. He's tall. With gentle eyes and a square jaw … and slender."

"What kind of shoes are you wearing?" Sandy asks.

A strange question. In my mind's eye I look down.

"Sandals. Brown ones. He's wearing them, too." And now I am the woman wearing brown sandals. Me, but different. A different me. But I'm watching myself, like on a film screen. "We're wearing white belted robes, and my hair is long – two inches past my shoulders."

"What are you doing?"

"We're talking animatedly -- gesturing. We're happy to see each other. … Oh. We're scholars. I see us walking into a courtyard – it looks like a giant college campus. There's a breeze blowing and we see some people we know occasionally, and we wave, but I'm more interested in talking to Rob so we don't stop."

"Take me to the next scene. Jump ahead."

The picture dissolves in front of me and I search the horizon for something else. Way off I see a group of people and I zoom in on them.

"I'm with a group of people sitting on the floor of a library. We're cross-legged and talking about ideals, theories and beliefs. Someone else is talking right now and I keep catching Rob's eye across the circle," I say. I feel a great sense of belonging; I am a part of something.

"It's intellectually stimulating."

"Okay," Sandy says. "And now what about the next scene?"

Blackness. I'm alone in this space. I feel a presence to my right that is maybe Rob, but no one is there.

"I'm alone and very scared." I start to cry in real life, as me, in Sandy's room. But I don't open my eyes.

This is how it will feel. I hear a voice in my head. *This is what darkness and grief feel like. But it is okay to be alone.*

I tell Sandy what I heard and that I felt like it was coming from a higher presence. I can hear her writing this all down.

"Can you get a sense of when this time was? Or the time period from before?"

"I don't know when this was," I say.

"That's okay. I don't think it matters. I was just wondering," Sandy says. "Next scene – when you are ready to move there."

I wipe my tears and I hear, and then feel, Sandy push a tissue into my hand and place the box of them in my lap. I wipe my face and leave my eyes closed. I don't want to break this concentration, or relaxation, or whatever it is.

"It's the end of my life. Or near it. I'm lying in a bed."

"How old are you?"

"Fifties or sixties. A caretaker of some sort is looking after me. She's bringing something into the room and setting it down on the bedside table. Her hair is tied back in a band of fabric. I'm looking out the window and feeling regret and shame." My voice creaks and I hold my breath until the wave of sobs threatening to explode out of me is repressed enough that I can speak again. "I'm feeling pretty bad about myself. I let myself shrivel up after Rob's death. I didn't continue with my studies and I lost track of my other friends. I just holed up into myself and didn't live."

I succumb and am openly crying now. I breathe deeply into my tissue, covering my twisted mouth.

Sandy begins a visualization exercise with me. It seems I am to ask forgiveness from someone – or many someones, if need be.

"You seem to think that you've done this great wrong by not living after Rob died in this other life, so from whom will you ask forgiveness?" Sandy says.

The answers come immediately.

"First to Rob. For not carrying on without him. Then to God, for not being who I truly am. And then I must ask forgiveness from myself. For falling apart."

And so, in that order, Sandy leads me through the process. I approach Rob – for I know it's him, my friend in the other lifetime – and he puts his hand on my cheek. He smiles and tells me, "You just forgot who you were."

I next go before God to ask His forgiveness and I realize it is not needed. His forgiveness and love are always there.

When I go to forgive myself – this woman that died in the other lifetime – I get stuck.

"Ask her what's involved in forgiving her," Sandy says.

I ask, and the woman with chestnut hair says, "Remember your light. Realize what a fully magnificent being you are." This young woman who is me – the scholar woman that dies an early death – agrees to forgive herself, to learn. And then she tells me to not screw up this time. I laugh, but it's weird and catches in my throat, which hurts from holding back all the tears. I'm sure I've been here for hours. I'm exhausted.

"It's time to say good-bye to these people and to thank them for their help," Sandy says.

I say goodbye to all my friends and to this young woman, thanking her for helping me while helping herself, and I start to cry as I attempt to say goodbye to Rob. It's hard to do.

"What is your belief of death, Valerie? You. Your true essence, not your mind," Sandy asks.

I struggle with words I've heard before but don't seem to quite fit: a door, an adventure ... and I come across *a chance to grow and learn.*

"I know that I have been with Rob before; I was with him in this life and I'll see him again in the spirit world, and again in a following lifetime." My eyes are open now and I am in awe of the peace that I feel in this moment.

ON THE DRIVE BACK TO MARIA'S TO PICK UP AUBREY, I THINK ABOUT sadness – testing to see if I can feel both that and peace at the same time. I still have some residual sadness at Rob not being here with me now. And I'll continue to miss him, but I'm already better off in this life than I was when I passed out of that other life. Of this I'm sure. And I know that if I keep looking, I'll find out even more things about myself that I didn't know, or remember, from before.

CHAPTER 9

> *"When you gave me a hug yesterday, I was so stressed that I was starting to get a headache, and in less than a minute without saying a word you made me feel completely at peace and happy."*
> ~Rob; love letter excerpt

Praying to God, for me, is like talking to a friend's grandfather. I don't know him well, I'm afraid of saying the wrong thing and offending him and I don't really know what to talk about. The angels, on the other hand, are more approachable and so are easier to talk to. I believe this to be a result of my not praying enough, so when I get home from my past life regression, I sit and write out a prayer, letter style.

> Dear God,
> I feel I've been neglecting you. I'm sorry. Every blessing I have in my life is from you.
> Thank you for the beam of sunlight through the bathroom window the day Rob died. Thank you for Aubrey and the new soul inside me. Thank you for

Rob and the time I had with him. Thank you for Sandy and the peace she's guided me towards. Thank you for your angelic helpers who have given me so very much in these last months in terms of present peace. Also future peace.

Thank you for the regression you arranged (indirectly or directly), because what I saw gave me hope. Confidence. Peace. And calmness, too. I felt your presence, your eternal forgiveness, compassion, and love. I discovered a new truth about our purpose on this planet, and I was able to feel and speak to Rob again. Thank you so much for that.

I finally *know* I will see him again and I *know* that my life currently is already better then the end of my other one. I've already accomplished more. Thank you because I know you are a part of this as well.

Please help me to remember Who I Am. Please help me to remember that I am a magnificent being of light – just like everyone on Earth. Please help me to live up to my capabilities and …

Please help me to decide which coast to live on.

I pray this all in Jesus' name. Amen.

I READ BACK THROUGH MY LETTER PRAYER. *HMM*. THIS IS GETTING rather overdone. I think I'm obsessing a bit about this channeling – and probably anyone I talked to about this would think so as well. Do I really believe that the angels, or God, or Rob are speaking to me? Or is it just my Higher Self wising up and I'm finally taking the time to check in with myself? Well, even if I believed it was just me finally having some clarity and realizing a truth, where do I think that clarity is coming from?

I prayed, in my darkest of darkest hours, to a god I didn't even like and asked him for help. And now I have it. So, even if I don't believe the angels or whatever are directly sending me messages in answer to my questions, I can believe that they are sending me the clarity and power to figure out what I already know deep inside myself. It's the same thing really.

Time for another Sandy session. I'm sitting in the white wicker chair again and she is across from me on the couch. The sunroom's door is closed and a little white fluffball of a dog is yapping through the glass.

"I'm sorry," says Sandy. She gets up and puts the dog in a back bedroom with the door closed on it so the barking will not disturb us.

"May I do some Reiki on you?"

"What's that?" I ask through my tears. It seems that as soon as I walk through the door to Sandy's room, I am released from "being alright" and "handling it well" and I can finally let go and heal.

"It's a hands-on energy healing," she says, as she steps behind me and places her hands on my shoulders. I relax into them.

"What does Peace look like to you?" she asks.

I close my eyes.

"Like someone with their arms around me."

"And what does Fear look like?"

Fear has been showing up in my dreams as nightmares and during the day as Worry and Terror about everything. It seems I'm always scared these days. Like, I never used to be afraid to be alone in the house with just Aubrey. And I'm terrified my grief will somehow hurt the baby inside me, even though my midwife assured me that this was not an at-risk pregnancy.

"It's large and black. Like a tall shadow." I cower inside until I see Rob behind my closed lids. It doesn't really look like him, but

I know it is him just the same. He holds my hand and is beside me while I confront this shadow.

"Why is the shadow there?" Sandy asks. "What does it want? Who's face does it have?"

I squeeze Rob's hand and force myself to look up. I see, like in a movie, my eyes get wide. Confusion, Alarm, and finally a little bit of the Ridiculous flit through.

"Mine. It has my face," I say.

"Ah." Sandy walks around me to the couch and sits down again. I hear her write something on her paper. I leave my eyes closed.

There is silence in the sunroom.

"What are you doing now?" she asks.

"I'm asking the shadow for forgiveness for my anger at it. I'm angry at the fear because it's making me vulnerable and I don't like that." And then I see Rob. On the other side. Waiting for me. A soft chime goes off somewhere behind me.

"I'm walking through Fear's darkness now. Right through it. Rob's on the other side with a light." I chuckle. "It doesn't mean that I'm 'walking towards the light', as in death. It means I'm conquering the fear and finding the peace afterwards. With Rob."

I open my eyes and smile through tears.

I GO HOME AFTER PICKING AUBREY UP FROM MARIA'S AND WHEN I put her down for a nap, I write to Rob.

"Are you my guardian angel?"

No. If I was then you wouldn't have had one all this time and you do. He will be less involved right now because you won't need him as much. You have me right now. He will gradually come back into your life as you gradually do not need me as much.

"Thank you. That was beautiful to hear."

You are beautiful to look at.

I smile and breathe in deeply. I put away my journal and lay down in my bed, taking advantage of Aubrey's nap. As I lay there, I wonder about this new-found communication.

Aubrey wakes me from my nap by calling from her crib. I lift her out and change her diaper. I still feel so tired I want to cry. But I want to cry a lot these days, so I stuff the impulse and set my mind to slogging through the rest of the day. Usually I feel peace from Sandy's sessions but not today. Or maybe it was the abbreviated nap.

Aubrey and I go to the living room and I turn on Disney Channel. She heads to the toy box and I sit on the couch. I stare at the cartoons and begin listing the things that plague me. They appear, in my mind – bolded words floating in mid-air.

Fear. I fear bad things happening. I have viscous and ugly nightmares *while I'm awake* that frighten me and leave me edgy for days. I have no control over them and I look over my shoulder, literally, for evil spirits waiting to harm me.

I'm trying desperately to **live in the present**, but I don't know how. And it's especially hard when I randomly think of weird things like: If Rob becomes an angel, how can he be reincarnated again?

I'm so **overwhelmed** that all of life's decisions are mine alone now. None of them can be shared with Rob. My beautiful, sexy sounding-board is gone. And I've never had to attend to legal matters before. I am fraught with the fear of doing something wrong.

I guess I'm just **feeling sorry** for myself. I feel negative a lot, and I don't know if I should **move** to Oregon, or not. What if I move and I don't come back? Rob's grave is here.

Exhaustion. I think about exhaustion, too. Actually I'm just tired of thinking. But not doing it seems so irresponsible.

I pray for this turmoil to end, or at least to quiet down. Dear Angels, please do what you can and give me strength. Rob, please guide me if you are able.

"Mommy," Aubrey says and my attention is diverted to her.

"Yes?"

"Santa Claus is singing to Daddy." Her brown eyes look straight at me. And then just like that she shakes her head and laughs.

A lesson then. To not hold onto the madness, but to see the joy and reverence of life. Even if it seems shitty right now.

Aubrey is such a big girl. I see glimpses of "older her" emerging from "little her." Today she is wearing jeans and a ponytail on top of her head. She has a fleecy button-down sweater on with a leopard collar and cuffs. She looks five years old instead of her two.

I giggle to myself and I think to call Rob at work to tell him, and then remember I can't. My smile slips away, but then – just in time – Aubrey brings it back.

"Mommy, I need some coffee."

THINKING ABOUT OREGON AGAIN. I'M WORRIED ABOUT MY MOM. I think she's lonely. I know she wants me to move there. But Fernanda and Gerry and Lena would be severely bummed if I did. And I don't want to take Aubrey away from her cousins. Rob had so many cousins growing up. They were always around and some of his best friends were his cousins. I'd love that for Aubrey, too.

No matter what choice I make, I'll feel guilty for it.

IT'S AFTER CHRISTMAS NOW. IT'S AFTER I'VE GIVEN FERNANDA, LENA, and Gerry photo albums with copies of every picture I had of Rob. I knew it would be received with mixed emotions, but I also knew they'd want those pictures down the road.

I'm writing to Rob again. Writing him letters makes so much sense to me. I enjoy writing, and I love writing letters. So this is a great way to keep in touch with Rob. I smile to myself and the silliness, but slip into the sweetness anyway.

"Rob, I feel like I'm dishonoring you somehow. I'm afraid my attitude and acceptance to your death is bordering on disrespectful. My pride in my accomplishments – my growth through my grief – is it tacky?"

And then suddenly it wasn't a letter, but another conversation with him.

Are you kidding? Look at last time. Remember how bad you felt at the end? You didn't grow from your grief last time and you regretted it, you anguished. Think how much better you will feel at the end this time. Don't let others' beliefs or feelings dictate how you feel. Don't feel bad that you aren't reacting the way you perceive others' think you should feel.

I see the movie again; his hands are on my temples.

It's great to feel so alive here!

"I'm glad you are happy. It gives me an extra boost. Thank you for all that you've done – the dreams and such. Keep doing them."

You don't need them as much.

"What if you aren't my soulmate? Could I be so sure and still be wrong? If I fall madly in love with someone else, did I love you any less than I thought?"

Your love is eternal. I know it. I feel it. Always. In my heart and soul, never fear that. No critical mind here, think with your soul. And stay in the now.

I flash with annoyance. He keeps saying that.

You are hot-headed and stubborn. He says this fondly, but then gets serious. *Don't let that be your downfall.*

"I'm worried about so many things."

Find the peace and serenity of the moment.

I write, "Thank you for your words, direction and help tonight. Good night," because one must always be grateful to the spirits for communication. I feel grumbly and sad and thoughtful, so I go to sleep.

At Maria's two days later, Aubrey walks up to me in Maria's kitchen. I'm sitting at the table.

"I need Daddy," Aubrey says.

"I know you need Daddy, but he's far away," I say.

"No he's not. He's in the ground."

My heart stops.

"Who told you that, Sweetie?" Maria and I look at each other.

Her response is rather unintelligible but I hear: car, Daddy, and hit.

"Who told you that?" I repeat.

"Aubrey," she says. My heart is thumpity thumping. Kids know so much. The veil is so much thinner for them. They can see spirits and hear them much clearer than adults can. Was Rob talking to her, too? Did she have conversations with him, too?

"Who told you that, Aubrey?"

"Jake." Jake is Maria's dog. Hmm. I try one more time.

"Who told you that?"

"Daddy." Jackpot. Or maybe I was just leading her to say it with my repeated question.

"What else did Daddy tell you?"

Nothing. All I got was juicebox and chair. But still. Maybe he *was* bringing her some peace, too. I certainly hope so. Maria and I look at each other with hopeful eyes.

Later that evening, Aubrey returned to the old conversation.

"Daddy's far away, in the air. He sees us," she says. But I think maybe this is just her repeating what I'd told her before.

It's a Sunday morning and I'm in the kitchen with Aubrey. We're in our jammies, snacking. Fernanda bustles around the downstairs, and every so often she comes upstairs to her bedroom and rustles around in there. She finds us in the kitchen on one of her walk-throughs.

"Aren't you going to church this morning?" she says.

I shrug my shoulders and scrunch up my nose.

"Nah. I don't think so."

She stares at me.

"Well, what about Aubrey?"

I look at my baby girl who is two years old and full of sparkle and laughter. She's sitting up tall in her booster seat, munching, and I suddenly want to snuggle and play with her all day. I don't want her to go with Fernanda this morning.

"Nah," I repeat. I smile at Aubrey. "I think I'll keep her home with me today." I pretend to tickle her cheeks.

Fernanda doesn't say anything. I look up at her from the table; she's standing in the doorway from the hall.

"But …" she splutters. "She needs to go to church."

"I think it's okay if she misses it, Fernanda."

She's angry now. I can see it. But really, why? Religion is such a nuisance. I feel closer to God now than I ever have and church has had nothing to do with it.

"Her father would want you to take her!"

Wow.

As if she knew what Rob is thinking right now.

I extricate myself, with Aubrey, from the conversation and hide in the back bedroom that houses our "living room" until she leaves.

How dare she.

I start fuming and then realize that I really don't have to stand for her instructing me about how I should raise Aubrey, and her cleaning up after me like I don't know how.

I could just move to Oregon.

Then she wouldn't be privy to whether I went to church, or brought Aubrey, or baptized the new baby, or had Aubrey go to that communion wedding dress thing when she's in first grade, or whatever.

And suddenly this seems like the best idea in the world. I pace back and forth between the two rooms at the end of hall that Aubrey and I claim as our own. I look in the "living room" at

Aubrey, watching her play, as I walk back and forth talking to myself.

Of course this is best. Rob and I had wanted to move to our own place anyway, so I've actually been thinking of doing this for a year. I get more and more excited with the thought of seeing my Mom every week – *or every day!* – and having the children love her as much as Aubrey loves Fernanda.

I remembered when Aubrey was a baby, seven months old maybe, and was sitting on the floor in our living room. The baby gate was up in the hallway and Fernanda was walking towards it cooing hello to her. Aubrey held up her arms and flailed her chubby fingers open and closed. "Ah ah ah," she said, reaching and smiling to Fernanda for her to pick her up. I wanted Aubrey to scramble for my mom, too. Moving to Oregon would bring them closer together and Mom could also be at the new baby's birth.

I slow my pacing. But what if I go to Oregon and I like it too much? I'll make friends and maybe meet a man to share my life with. Then I wouldn't ever come back to Massachusetts as I plan to.

Massachusetts is comfort. Gerry invites me to dinners so I don't have to eat alone with Aubrey, Lena babysits so I can get out to the confidence workshop I go to once a week, and other friends go walking in state parks with me, take me out to the movies, and invite me and Aubrey over for playdates so I am occupied away from my thoughts. And Maria! Maria invited me to her place last Christmas to celebrate.

Our children had played and we had had dinner, and I was accepted. Not as a couple, but just me. I was plagued only once with a melancholy moment that night – Maria's husband coming up to me after dinner. I was watching the kids play while Maria cleaned up the table and he walked up beside me with his hands in his jeans pockets. He rolled on his toes – his white socks against the wine colored plush carpet.

"I can't even imagine it, Valerie," he said.

I hadn't said anything in response – just looked at Aubrey and pressed my lips together in a sad smile. He didn't expect one anyway. His words were the only way he could say he was sorry. It had been his way of reaching out and figuratively holding my hand.

And I am still grateful for that. Still grateful that I have friends and loving family all together in one place. Sandy is here, too.

But if I work hard with her for the rest of the time I'm here – because it would be important to move before the baby was born – I could have a good steady base. One that might withstand a couple of bumps, and then find someone in Oregon to receive more one-on-one therapy. But how do I find this person? I felt kind-of *led* to find Sandy. Maybe that will happen again.

During that first past-life regression I did with Sandy, I discovered that I took the *easy* way out and suffered greatly. Instead of strengthening my character, I opted to close myself off and didn't grow anymore. This time I am determined not to follow suit.

Oh God.

If Rob died in the last life and I didn't grow, and he died again in this life to give me another opportunity to learn and live (because so far that's the only good that's come out of his death) ... then, wouldn't I have been the indirect cause of Rob's death?

I stop still as a statue. If I could see my face, it would be white. I know it. I lean against a wall in the hallway and slide down, wrapping my arms around my knees. I gasp and fight the urge to cry in front of Aubrey.

"Mommy?" She toddles over and hands me her toy. I look at her. Her hair is getting long. I put it in braids today. My throat convulses and my ears pop. Never mind, I tell myself. Just keep moving. One foot in front of the other. Do it. For Aubrey. For the new baby.

I force a smile and take the toy from Aubrey. I crawl into the living room, herding Aubrey in front of me like a Border Collie. She shrieks with delight and runs ahead of me to the center of the room. I sit next to her and hand her the toy and she scampers off to get a new one from the toy box to tempt me into another game.

Aubrey searches the depths of the toy box and finds nothing to suit her. She heads to the desk, to *her* drawer, and brings back a coloring book and some crayons.

Sandy says that choices and decisions are never wrong because you will still learn something from the endeavor. I can believe that. Also, moving to Oregon isn't the last decision I'll ever make. I can always make another decision to come back. It doesn't have to be permanent.

What if we leave and I don't continue working on my soul work? I've had problems with self-discipline in the past. I'd hate to quit while I was ahead and un-do what has finally been done.

I take out a green crayon and start in on a tree. Aubrey's gaze is intent. She never joins me, only watches me do all the work.

Oregon would be starting over. Which is good, but also exhausting to the point of tears. Oregon would be me relying on myself. Which would make me stronger.

Massachusetts would be the easy way out; it wouldn't ruffle any feathers. But I don't feel free to make decisions here. I'm afraid of losing my voice here.

I hand Aubrey a blue crayon and try to coax her into joining me. She abstains and looks at the TV.

I think I may have just made up my mind. By choosing Oregon, I am not shutting out the people and memories in Massachusetts – and I'm not locking myself in. I can always come back and it won't be a waste of time to do this. I'd still be learning.

I smile. I feel jittery – yet relieved.

CHAPTER 10

> "God, I love you. ... I don't know why but I still can't shake that fear that I'm gonna lose you. Maybe it's because you seem too good to be true. I don't know. I only know that I love you, and that I'll be yours for as long as you'll have me."
> ~Rob; love letter excerpt

"I've decided to move."

There it is. The bombshell I've been afraid to share with the family. Fernanda is folding clothes. She stops and looks at me with dismay, and maybe a little fear. I would be taking her last link to Rob, if I left. Her grandbabies, Rob's children. Gone. Just like him. She puts down the toddler shirt she's folding. She is speechless.

"I miss my mom." I smile, trying to make light. "She didn't get to be at Aubrey's birth; I'd like her to be at this baby's." I hold my belly and sit down across the table from her, the laundry between us. I sigh, and wonder how to explain this.

"Rob and I had been talking about moving for a long while now," I say. "And I've wondered whether to do it and *when* to do it – before or after the baby's born. But I miss my mom and I want to be with her. I want my kids to know *my* mom, too, like Aubrey knows you."

She blinks and looks at her hands that are still resting on the shirt. She pulls them to her lap slowly, like all of a sudden they weigh more than they ever have before. She has sturdy, firm hands. Hands that have washed clothes, and cooked, and bathed bodies. Hands that have sewn curtains in factories, and Halloween costumes for her grandchildren. Weathered hands. Rough hands. Lovely hands.

"Everybody's different," she says. I think she says this when she doesn't know what else to say. I think she says it when she can't fathom the thoughts and actions of others.

I tilt my head at her, begging with my eyes for her to understand me because my words would only end in tears.

"I want you to be happy," she says. She gasps then, and presses her fingers to her lips.

I flash to our conversation about the funeral pyre where she'd done the same thing. *Weren't Catholics cremated?* I was able to give her what she wanted then, but I couldn't now. I couldn't stay here now.

"I only want you to be happy," she says again. She stands abruptly and walks to the sink.

My heart beats heavy and fast in my chest, though it feels more like it's slipped down in my stomach, bobbing around in there, out of place. There are so many other reasons why I want to move, but none that I can share with anyone except Maria.

I'M AT MARIA'S AGAIN. AUBREY AND MARIA'S SON ARE WATCHING A cartoon video and dancing. Maria and I are laughing ourselves silly. We pull out our cameras and take pictures of the kids while they dance – Aubrey's diaper slipping down in the back – renewing our hysterics. It feels good to laugh. And Maria is the only person I feel comfortable laughing in front of. With any of the others: Fernanda, Lena, Gerry, Stacey … it all feels wrong.

Like I should be ashamed of myself for finding delight in anything.

I sigh the sigh you do after laughing so much your sides hurt, and wipe the tears from my eyes. We giggle a bit more and I tuck my camera away.

"I think it's time I move, Maria."

"Aww." Maria's response is disappointed but she still nods with acceptance. She's known it was coming. I'd been talking about it for weeks.

"I need to be allowed to grieve the way I know is best for me, and I can't do that here with Rob's family." I brush my pants and rub my knuckles. "They'll take care of me for the rest of their lives, and I'll never grow." I look up. "Can you imagine me trying to date anyone with them around? I mean, when the time comes." I pause and then shake my head. "It'd be stabbing them in the heart. A betrayal they'd never forgive. At least if I move away, they don't have to watch it. They'll just know about it from afar."

Maria watches me, but doesn't say a word.

"I can't be alone for the next sixty years. I don't imagine that that's what's supposed to happen." I am a little defiant with my voice. I'm not trying to convince Maria, but myself.

ANOTHER PAST LIFE REGRESSION WITH SANDY. I'M WEARING HIKING boots and jeans, a ripped tee-shirt and a flannel. I feel male in this life, with straight black hair that just brushes my shoulders. I think it's night; everything is quiet and I'm looking for something. I'm a little bit cold. I fumble with a cigarette and feel the beginnings of hunger. Mostly I'm apprehensive. Waiting.

"What are you doing now?" Sandy asks.

"I'm walking. Trying to keep warm."

"Where are you?"

"I'm walking down some train tracks."

Sandy's pen writes and her cuff drags across the paper.

"And now?" she says after a few moments.

She keeps her voice low and slow, I know, because she wants me to remain in my "trancy" state. To not jostle me out of where I am. But I'm still here in this sunroom, too. Weird. I don't want to drift too far away from this other life, so I turn my mind inward again.

"I'm sitting at a table now. It's a big family turkey dinner. I don't feel like I fit in. I keep looking at them to see what they do."

"Who's there, at the table?" Sandy says.

In my mind I turn my face to the left and look across the table from me. Maybe I did it in the present tense, too, so that Sandy could see.

"There's a younger girl – ten or eleven. She's sitting next to her brother. He's seventeen or eighteen. The father is balding … he's at the head of the table. He looks kind and stern at the same time. And the mother is a homey-type. She's wearing an apron."

Sandy doesn't say anything. She lets me look around and see what's important in the scene.

"I'm drawn to the son – the teenager. He's quick to laugh and seems compassionate. He reminds me of Rob – only what he might have been like at a younger age."

"There's one more person at the table. She's not saying much, just happy to be there taking it all in. She looks wise – probably the grandmother. I feel drawn to her, too," I say.

"How did these people find you?" Sandy asks.

"I don't remember. It must've had to do with the son."

More moments pass.

"I get the sense – like a feeling – that I can belong here. They're willing to accept me, if I allow myself to be accepted."

"Where is your – this boy's – family?" Sandy says.

"If they're around, they're of no consequence. I'm not sure. He feels alienated for some reason."

"Okay. Let's move forward in his life."

I let the scene dissolve behind my eyes and wait with open soul. A new scene materializes, like Spock and Bones being beamed aboard the USS Enterprise.

"He has a dog now. He's starting to heal. He laughs a little now. He's around twenty. The family that took him in helped him. He was an important person to them." *I was an important person to them.*

"I wonder about his past. Why he was alone before? Do you know anything about his family?" Sandy says.

"Um." I check the records. It's literally like looking back through my own memories to find his – which are really mine after all, because I am him and he is me. "His father's an alcoholic. The family doesn't understand the boy. They're always fighting and he decides to leave. His parents drain all his energy. He doesn't want to be a part of that anymore. He doesn't feel good about himself when he's with them."

I gasp.

"What?" Sandy asks.

"The mother is my sister." I can see the disapproving set of my sister's face – from this life – superimposed on my mom's face – from that life.

"What about the father? Do you know him?"

It doesn't jump out at me at once, like the mother figure did. But I think he might be my first husband. Of course, now I doubt myself, since the answer was slow in coming.

"What was this regression of yourself like, as a boy?" she goes on.

"Sad. He hid the sadness from others, though. Didn't let it overwhelm him, but it kept him blocked from the universal energy all around us."

I must've lagged in the conversation because Sandy has to prompt me.

"What are you seeing now?"

"I think he's dying," I say. "Of cancer. Because of his sadness. It blocked him. The sadness blocked him and the cancer came and starting growing from the blockages."

"How old is he?"

"Around sixty. He still feels alone." I wonder about the age sixty. I died in that scholarly lifetime at sixty, too. I wonder if this in an important age for me.

"What do you need to know here?"

"Cleansing." I nod to myself, as if clarifying. "Cleansing internally and spiritually – letting go of the past hurts, so your energy isn't blocked." I smooth my shirt down over my growing belly with my eyes still closed. "It makes you healthier."

"I want you to visualize the father and mother reuniting with him in Spirit."

I do.

"From the soul's perspective, is there any forgiveness needed?"

"No." My voice is soft and calm. "I feel happy for them. They can now be whole. And there is love flowing again." I pause and let my mind take me where it wants to go. I figure my soul knows what I need to experience right now, so I give it full reign. I'm in a safe place.

"My soul is telling me to be thankful for the people in my life. Even though I might not have a good relationship with them. That it's all part of the play." I think of my sister again.

I wait to see if that is all. Sandy thinks this is enough time spent here and talks me back to the room. I blink in the bright room and breathe deeply. It seems that when I trance I breathe shallowly, because I always take a deep breath afterwards.

I pay her, make an appointment for the following week and then drive back to Maria's to pick up Aubrey. Maybe we'll drink some tea while I tell Maria about my session.

Past life regressions are getting easier. I don't even need to be hypnotized to access them. But maybe that just speaks to my ability to get relaxed quickly.

I'll miss this when I move to Oregon. And then I feel a little surge of panic. *What if I can't do this there? Can I do it alone, without Sandy to help me? What if I lose this connection to Rob?* Because that's what it is. Being able to access the spirit world gives me access to Rob. Doing past life regressions gives me back Rob. I see him again in the other characters of the past lives I remember, and it reminds me that I'll be with him again in another life. And that makes the pain bearable. It's not permanent. I'll see him again.

AUBREY STARTS HAVING TROUBLE SLEEPING AT NIGHT. IT TAKES HER A long time to fall asleep and she's been having nightmares. I buy her a book of meditations for children and she promptly dubs them "Dreaming Stories." The first meditation in the book is called "Animals." We start with that one.

The lights are out in her room, but I leave the hall light on so I can read by it. I move a chair into her room and sit next to her bed. She closes her eyes and listens, with her chubby toddler fingers resting on top of her body over the covers. Her dark Portuguese lashes contrast her pale clear skin and I want to kiss her cheeks but don't. I don't want to interrupt her thoughts and the pictures in her mind's eye. If I touch her, she'll pull out of her relaxation.

Afterward we talk about what she saw.

"What did you see with your eyes closed, Aubrey?"

"A tree ... tall ... with bugs."

"Do they live there?" I ask.

"Yes. And a frog lives in the tree, too. I climb on his back and he gives me a ride."

"Hop hop hop," I say.

"Hop hop hop," she repeats in her angel voice.

"What else did you see?"

"A horse. He was crying."

"Aww. Why?"

"Because it wanted a *beeka*," she says. Ah. Our word for pacifier.

"Was it a baby horse?"

"Yes."

"The baby horse is happy now. Did he say thank you?" I ask.

"Yes. He's happy because Aubrey gave him the *beeka* and he

did say thank you," Aubrey says. I smile in the dark at the lack of pronoun use.

I kiss her and say good night and stay with her until she falls asleep.

I think these meditations will be great for her creativity and ability to relax and visualize. I think it'll help her concentration, too, for when she starts school. It also re-iterates to her that she is special to me because I choose to spend time doing this with her, bonding. And I hope she'll find it easier to remember that she's not alone and that her nightmares won't be as frequent because she'll have some special place to go to in her dreams.

"I love you, Aubrey," I whisper before leaving the room.

My feet are cold so I go into my room for my slippers. They aren't there. *Hmm.* I check the living room and the bathroom. I wander down to the parlor where the computer is, too, thinking maybe I took them off while sitting at the desk. Not there. On a mission now – to find my slippers – I go back to my room where they should be but aren't, and look again. Still not there.

I look under the bed. Nope.

I look under the crib. Nope.

I look behind the door. Nope.

And finally.

I look in the closet, where I would never put them in a million years, and there they are.

I force my shoulders down from my ears but I'm not able to unclench my jaw or un-press my lips. My head tingles in frustration. *Fernanda.*

She put them here.

Again.

I had told her I didn't like them in the closet. They're more accessible to me neatly placed by my bedroom door. I wear them everyday, and being hugely pregnant makes it hard to bend over to find them at the bottom of the closet. I want to just slip them on or off as I walk in and out of my bedroom. *My* bedroom. *My* slippers.

"But they look ugly there," she had said. Totally ignoring my request to leave them where they were.

And now she's done it again.

Come into my room and put my slippers away and made my bed.

And she finishes my dishes, too. I'll start to load the dishwasher and Aubrey will need my attention so I'll stop mid-task and I'll come back hours later to the whole kitchen being clean.

I know on some level that I will look back on this and appreciate it someday. I mean who wouldn't like someone doing your laundry and dishes for you. But right now? It feels like a *giant* invasion of my privacy.

I scoff and snatch the slippers out of the closet and force my feet into them. My face tightens and stretches into angry lines. *Privacy?* This isn't even my home really. It's Fernanda's.

CHAPTER 11

> *"It's not even 11pm yet and I feel like I'm gonna die if I don't see you. I better go to bed so I can at least dream about you. I wonder, do you dream about me? Goodnight, Carida (Sweetheart)."*
> ~Rob; love letter excerpt

I'm soaking up all the opportunities I can to heal with Sandy before I move, so I enroll in a class Sandy and her friend are teaching based on a book called "Journey Home." It's a parable about a man who meets different angelic helpers on a journey, and receives gifts from them. I tell Fernanda it's a class to build confidence, which is true ... in a way. Lena watches Aubrey while I go, so I don't feel guilty going.

One evening, all of us in the class sit on the hardwood floor in a sunroom. We're in a circle. The homework for last week was to bring in something that we want to let go of. Something significant. We're learning about the folly of placing importance in material things. How we sometimes assign emotional importance to an object and it becomes way too critical to us. In a disproportional way. We were to bring it in to today's session and *leave it.*

This seems a bit harsh to me. I mean, come on. It's something really important to you. Why would you want to, or frankly be able to, send it packing?

Of course they're right. But I've forgotten to bring anything. Mostly because I don't do that sort of thing – place importance on material objects. I'm not materialistic, and things are things. I don't give them intrinsic value. We got the assignment, I felt it didn't apply to me, so I promptly forgot all about it.

After the candle in the center of our circle is lit, and we go around and talk about the reading and journaling we did during the week, the rest of the workshop participants bring out their objects and one at a time start telling about them. They are emotional stories full of beauty and pain and ... are really so *interesting*. One woman has a serving dish that represents popularity to her. One man has a laminated card that he's kept in his wallet for four years.

I feel bad that I haven't brought something. These people have all done the proper soul-searching and put in the decent amount of time and energy that is required by this assignment. And I ... have brought nothing. I feel like I've cheated somehow. When it's my turn to talk, I can't just say, "I didn't bring anything because I don't have this problem that the rest of you seem to have." That would be rude. And maybe not even true.

Do I place importance in material objects? Do I infuse them with power and trap emotions inside them so they beat frantically and mercilessly to get out, like a moth caught in the light fixture on my ceiling?

It's still chilly in the sunroom. There is a towel by the back door to catch the snow dripping off our shoes as we walked in and removed them. I put my hands in my coat pockets to settle in and listen to the person across the circle from me speak. My hand nestles around the unopened cigarette pack in the right-hand pocket. It's a comfort to me. I often hold it in my hand like this. Like I'm holding Rob's hand. Because these are Rob's cigarettes.

And then I stop.

Frozen.

Not breathing.

I clap my hand to my mouth and my breath crashes out in a sob.

This is the thing.

I *do* do this.

I *do* place emotional import in material objects. This packet of cigarettes has been in my pocket for seven months. I have been holding the pretend hand of a dead man for *seven months*.

When it is my turn to talk, I place my packet of cigarettes in the center of the circle with shaking hands and voice. And I tell my story. Again.

THE DAYS ARE CHAOTIC WITH MOVING PREPARATIONS. AUBREY SPENDS most of the time downstairs now with her little cousin. She's six months younger than Aubrey, and though she is 100% Portuguese, she has surprisingly golden blond hair. The girls play together well – building Lego towers to knock down and watching *Bear in the Big Blue House* and *The Wiggles*. But today I have friends over to help me pack stuff in boxes and Aubrey is upstairs with me and my friends' toddlers.

I hired a moving company to pick everything up in a couple of days and I'm frantically trying to get it all finished. Another company is picking up my car, and a big semi-trailer will tow it across the country along with shelves of other cars. I'm surprised at how inexpensive it is. Flying to Oregon with Aubrey will be much more relaxing than driving a U-Haul, towing my car behind, and stopping every hour and a half to accommodate Aubrey's bathroom and food needs. Also, just considering her desire to not be sitting in her car seat for two days straight. Frankly, *I* have that desire, too, so the airplane it is.

And we are old hats at flying back and forth between Oregon and Massachusetts. We've visited my parents many times.

Maria is here with her son. Aubrey and he are in ecstasy playing together. I've left Aubrey's toys and books to pack for last.

Another friend from our birthing class is over, too, with her daughter that looks so much like Aubrey. Our three kids are all roughly the same age, and Maria and I have discovered just today that our friend is pregnant again, too. All three of us pregnant again at the same time! We laugh and hug and cry and promise to stay in touch.

After hours of boxing and taping, the rooms begin to look like a garden after harvest – sparse and picked through. Discarded pieces I've decided not to bring with me like colorless, dried weeds. I feel the tense-in-my-belly excitement of an adventure. Oregon will give me so much. I will grow and live and heal … and grieve. I know I'm not running away from that.

THE DAY WE LEAVE, LENA DRIVES US TO THE AIRPORT. IT'S FEBRUARY and cold. My belly is huge now. I'm eight months pregnant. As crazy as it is moving when I'm eight months pregnant, I figure it would have been worse trying to do it *after* the baby came. I'd have so much more to move! Including an extra body.

Lena waits with me until our flight is called to board. She hands me a yellow envelope and hugs me hard.

"Don't open it until you get on the plane and you're flying," she says.

Lena and I both hold back our tears and force out flight attendant smiles and talk to Aubrey about the grand adventure we are going on. Aubrey's pack has been lovingly padded with coloring books and new fat crayons and yummy snacks.

We all hug again and say good-bye. Aubrey and I walk onto the airplane and prepare to *start again*. We'll be moving into an apartment that my mom has arranged for us not too far away from her. In fact, she and Dad are actually splitting up after twenty-nine years (ten years too late in my opinion; neither of them have been happy for a long time), and she'll be moving into the same apartment complex. So we'll be neighbors. At least until I find a house to buy. I've never bought a house before. What if I make a rotten mistake and buy something that gets me into real financial trouble later on? The houses in Oregon are *way* cheaper than those in Massachusetts, though, so that brings me a little bit more confidence.

I have Social Security Survivor Benefits for Aubrey and myself – and I'll get more when the baby is born – and I receive something called DIC income from the Department of Veteran's Affairs because Rob was technically on active duty when he died. That will be enough monthly income to live on, even with a new mortgage payment. Also, I have Rob's life insurance money. That will give me a good down payment on anything I find. I also don't want a car payment, so I had made arrangements to pay off my car before I left Massachusetts.

I sigh down past my belly-button. So much to have to think about. It never stops. There is no reprieve. And no one to pass the reigns to when I am tired.

We find our seats and I get Aubrey all settled. We buckle up and I pull out Lena's card. I tear open the yellow envelope. She knows of my recent interest in angels (I'm wearing the blue angel pendant she gave me for Christmas); the card is in this theme, too. I cry at the poetry as I read and especially at Lena's addition: *I love you, Valerie. Take care of yourself and kiss that beautiful angel every night for me. Love ALWAYS, Lena.*

Lena didn't always love me. She never let me know though. When I first met her, she chatted amiably and drove Rob and I around in her black Ford Bronco. We smoked cigarettes together and talked about her job at Lenscrafters. I never knew she was mad at me for stealing Rob away from her. That was how she put it when she finally told me.

On the day of Rob's death, I had been kneeling in the living room floor. I think I was looking for clothes to give to Gerry. Already divvying up pieces of Rob to give away. "Valerie?" Lena had walked down the hall towards me, Fernanda shadowing behind her at a distance. I looked up at Lena's curly black hair.

She shoved her hands into the pockets of her jeans. "I want to apologize to you." She gasped and held her breath.

I dropped what I was doing and stood up.

"Why?" I started to cry again when I saw her tears.

"Because I was so mad at you." She sobbed and scrubbed at her face, like she was trying to wipe away the memory. "When Rob came back from the army *married*, I was so mad. Like you'd taken him away from us. From *me*." She choked again and I held out my arms to her. She shook her head and stayed in the hallway.

"But when I came in from outside just now, I saw the note on the refrigerator door. The one he wrote that says he misses you? I knew then, *after all this time...*" – she shook her head again – "...that he *loved* you. And I just want to say thank you for giving him that. Giving him your love and allowing him to feel that love for you in return. Thank you."

Fernanda had stepped forward then and had pulled Lena into a hug. Only after that, had Lena allowed herself a hug from me.

"Mommy, why are you crying?"

Busted. I smile and laugh at myself. I wipe away the tears.

"Because I'm happy at the pretty card, *Ti-tia* gave me." But she knows I'm sad. She distracts easily with a sippy cup of juice, and I surround myself with a blanket of Lena's love and know that if Oregon doesn't work out, we will always have a home and welcoming arms in Massachusetts.

PART II

Smell the Blue Sky

(Oregon)

CHAPTER 12

> *I'm so glad I still see you in my dreams, my love.*
> *~me*

It had been seven months since Rob died, one month since I'd moved, and I hated this ugly March day. I felt needy. I craved companionship. I was lonely AND I wanted to be alone. I honored this part of my journey, I really did. I knew I needed to feel this shitty part now, in order to learn self-sufficiency. To learn how to feed myself. To learn that I was interesting alone. That I didn't need someone telling me that.

Except that I wanted that someone.

I didn't mind being alone, really, if I was truly alone. Trying to keep Aubrey occupied while my brain rotted on cartoons until I was ready to go insane was not alone. I just wanted quiet. I wanted to hear myself think. I wanted to sit and write or cry. I wanted to take a hot bath without being interrupted.

And then I thought of the alternative, and I was so grateful she was here.

Fernanda had been a buffer. When things got too much, I had Aubrey play downstairs with Fernanda and I took a break. But I severed that option for myself when I moved to Oregon. Like I knew it would. It just felt more ... *acute* right then.

I decided to treat myself to a bath that night. I was chilly and the water would warm me. In fact, I was so looking forward to Aubrey being in bed that I sped-read her a short picture book and gave her a peck on the cheek instead of taking my time with her. I hurried and ran the water before she'd actually fallen asleep and got in, hoping she'd manage it on her own. I really needed that bath.

I should've known better. Where was my mommy intuition when I needed it?

I didn't even know why I was surprised. I didn't enjoy the bath. The tub wasn't deep enough for the water to cover my eight-months-pregnant belly, so I was cold, and because she was still awake, the room wasn't absent enough of Aubrey noises for me to relax, nor write. I got out of tub and yelled at her to get back to bed, and then sat in the tepid water and listened to her cry while I tried not to cry myself. *Epic fail.*

Her hair was still sticking to her tear-stained face when I checked on her after getting out of the bathtub. I hated yelling at her. I felt sick when I succumbed to it. Thankfully, for both of us, it didn't happen often.

I climbed into bed and turned on my lamp, beaten. I pulled out my journal, still hoping to get a chance to write before falling asleep. But after dozing with the lamp on, I just turned it off and put my journal away.

I needed Aubrey to go to sleep by herself. I couldn't be with her every night. Once I delivered, I'd need to be with the baby sometimes – a *lot* of the times. If Rob were here, he could go to her ... I closed my eyes in the darkness of the room and the sickness of giving up grew inside me like a cancer.

Aubrey woke before six in the morning and was in a crappy mood, *poor dear*, setting the stage for another terrible day for the both of us. I prayed that tomorrow would be better. Again – for both of us. I just felt so fed up, defeated – like I needed to recuperate from something.

Turns out it was more like *rest up* for something.

Fifteen days later my baby was born.

Around six in the morning my contractions were obvious; I called my mom to pick us up. I grabbed my hospital bag and a backpack for Aubrey with things she might need. Mom and I dropped Aubrey off at a friend's house and then Mom drove me to the hospital.

I checked in, changed my clothes into a gown and socks, and my midwife looked in on me. Then we made ourselves comfortable. Mom read and worked on her laptop. A nurse came in and asked me something about a blood test I was supposed to have taken earlier. I didn't recall getting one so they took a blood sample and came back later with antibiotics and an IV bag. It seemed I had Strep B, which had no symptoms for me, but could do whopping damage to the baby as it comes through the birth canal -- even death. *Lovely.*

I walked, got in and out of the bathtub, lay down and breathed. I gave myself Reiki and sucked on ice chips. I lasted as long as I could without drugs. The nurse said that was silly.

"If you had a headache, you'd take a pill, right? This is a baby. It hurts more than a headache. Take the medication. It won't hurt the baby."

I took the drugs. I put on my headphones and listened to soothing music with no lyrics. I faded in and out of sleep and saw beautiful warped colorful tracers behind my eyes.

I wondered what kind of drugs I'd been given.

When they wore off, it was time for the epidural.

And then pushing.

And then the birth.

That my mom attended. And not Rob.

I appreciated that my mom was there. But still. Last time, for

Aubrey's birth, he held my hand, and paced around the room, and tried not to punch the anesthesiologist for missing the vertebral pocket and hitting a nerve on his first attempt to give me the epidural. Rob pushed on my back and cut the cord and kissed me and watched everything the team did with our baby girl. He slept on a cot in my room until I went home.

I had a healthy baby boy.

He was eight pounds and fourteen ounces. Almost nine pounds! Huge.

Rob and I had already picked out names before he died. Before I knew I was even pregnant. We'd been trying for eight months, so we'd had a lot of time to think about names.

Cheyenne Beth if it was a girl (Beth for a friend of his that had died earlier that year), and Joseph William if it was a boy. (Joseph for Rob's dad who died when Rob was three, and William for my dad.)

So there, at last, was my little Joseph William.

Joey.

But then, in a sudden burst of remembrance and grief-inspired nostalgia, I added Robert to the birth certificate. Robert Joseph William. I'd still call him Joey, but now he had a little piece of his daddy with him.

Mom had found us a ground floor apartment when we first moved over from Massachusettsback in February, so I didn't need to worry about the cement steps and babies falling and the scraped knees they'd have if we had a second floor apartment.

It was a two bedroom, so Aubrey had her own room and I set up a bassinette in mine for Joey. Hopefully I'd have a bigger house by the time I needed to set up the crib.

I had modestly decorated the apartment with just the need-to-haves, knowing that I'd spend more time, and money, making a place characteristically *mine* once I bought a house. For now, a green squishy couch, a little table to eat off of, a new dresser for Aubrey, and new beds was all I needed. I was using my great-grandmother's old bedstead and dresser and I finally had back in my possession my favorite of her pieces, her vanity table with the big round mirror. I hadn't seen it since I'd joined the army four years earlier.

When I first moved in, my dad -- ever the handyman – *stapled* the phone cord all across the living room ceiling to the outlet so I could get internet. I was both horrified at how ugly and tacky it was, and grateful.

Our living room housed a big glass sliding door out to the center grassy yard that all of the tenants in our complex shared. There was a play-structure just outside that I took Aubrey to as often as I had energy. She sorely missed her cousins and playmates. She was bored a lot. She liked the ducks, though. They waddled up to our little patio and stared in the window.

ONE MORNING MY CELL PHONE RANG. I USED IT MORE NOW THAN I ever had before. It used to only be in my glove compartment for emergencies on the road and I left it turned off. Now it was always on and family from back East called us on it.

Today it was Lena. We chatted for a bit and then she wanted to talk to Aubrey.

I handed Aubrey the phone.

"It's *Ti-tia*. She wants to talk to you and say hello."

I went about my tasks and plodded around the kitchen while Aubrey sat at the table on the phone. I smiled every time I looked over. Such a big girl. *On the phone.* Just like a teenager – I stifled a laugh – but so not. She had a ponytail high on her head and was wearing blue corduroy overalls over a shirt with ruffles at the cuffs and collar. She was so intent on the conversation, she looked grown-up. With blue overalls. I shook my head again at the juxtaposition.

Aubrey found me at the table on another day.

"A ghost bit my hand," she said.

I frowned. That didn't seem right.

"No, it didn't, honey. Ghosts aren't mean, they're just sad and lonely."

"Yeah, he misses his mommy." She crawled into my lap for a hug.

I nestled my chin over her head.

"And I miss my friends in Massachusetts," I thought.

I swung my knees side to side and rocked Aubrey back and forth. My thoughts drifted. I was so glad that I did everything right with Rob. I wouldn't have changed anything. We parted on good terms, and there was no guilt involved for any of our life together. He wasn't perfect and I certainly wasn't either. But we made a difference in each other's lives, and for that I was grateful.

CHAPTER 13

 *Joey laughed today and I turned to tell you.*
~me

Joey was one month old. It was Mother's Day 2001. My sister was getting married and I'd be traveling to Kentucky in a few months to be in her August wedding. Before that we'd be in Massachusetts to visit Fernanda, Gerry and Lena and everyone else. It'll be great to see them all again, but uber-weird and chokingly sad that the trip would be right during the one year anniversary of Rob's death.

I had stopped wearing our wedding rings around my neck by then. It seemed less morbid to wear mine now though, if I wanted to, and for a while I contemplated wearing it on my right hand but that could confuse a potential suitor so I hadn't done it. I wished that our culture still wore black mourning clothes. It seemed a much simpler way to deal with grief. You wouldn't have to explain anything; you wouldn't have to worry about wearing your wedding ring, or not. You wouldn't even have to worry about when to start dating again. It would be socially acceptable to effectively *blah* for one whole year. And no one could fault you for it. It would be expected of you. As long as you wore black, you were safe from having to make decisions or entertain people. You could do as you pleased.

I WAS GETTING READY FOR MY FAVORITE TV SHOW, *TOUCHED BY AN ANGEL*. I know, I know. It's lame and I didn't tell many people I watched it, but it brought me a little hope back then, which was something I hung on to in those days.

"Aubrey, it's time for nighty-night."

She wasn't ready.

I didn't want to just toss her to bed and hurry through our bedtime routine, like last time, so I abandoned it all together and let her lay on the couch with me. I saw her getting drowsy and I rubbed her back.

"Mommy," she whispered. "I need my diaper changed."

I pulled out the supplies and came back to the couch still watching the show. I took off the old diaper and cleaned her up. I started putting on the new diaper and she interrupted me.

"I need to go potty."

This was good news. She was almost potty-trained while we lived in Massachusetts, but then Rob died and I didn't stay on top of it. I wanted her to be able to go to pre-school in the Fall, and we only had four months to solidify it. I took her in the bathroom and left her to her "privacy" because the commercials were over and the show had started again.

On the couch my mommy ears eventually heard something peculiar. Splashing noises. Lovely. I scooted into the bathroom and found Aubrey playing in the toilet with the plunger.

"Poopy! Yuck, Aubrey!" I took the plunger from her and tapped her lightly on the butt. "Bad girl."

That was my mistake. Right there.

Bad Girl.

I never wanted those words to ever leave my lips. I didn't talk that way, and I certainly didn't believe the statement to be true. It was only the irritation, disgust in what she was playing with, and my surprise that it was happening at all. Though in retrospect I understood that she was only practicing what she'd seen others doing.

She fell completely apart and cried and cried while I cleaned up. She cried so much she was choking and gagging. I picked her up and carried her to bed and hugged her until she fell asleep.

I was so glad Joey didn't wake up through that.

ROB'S BIRTHDAY WAS COMING UP. I WANTED TO LIGHT A CANDLE FOR him. I thought it would be a nice ritual for Aubrey. She said a prayer to him the other night. She just talked about her doll and little stuff, but it was sweet and interesting. Fernanda still celebrated Rob's birthday. Her late husband's, too. She sent us money on those occasions.

I guess she did it because she couldn't give Rob and her husband a birthday present, so she gave Aubrey one instead. It was a little out of the ordinary ... but maybe not any more than lighting a candle.

DAYS OF HOUSE HUNTING, PREPPING FOR LESLIE'S WEDDING, preschool phone calls, and getting a driver's license so I could start school that summer filled my days. I poured through real estate magazines and considered my budget and called my realtor way more often than she probably wanted.

I'd looked at one house a couple of times – even brought my mom and sister once. I couldn't decide if I liked it enough to buy it.

"It doesn't have much character," I said to the realtor.

"You can *add* character."

She was right. And I was getting tired of looking. But was that a good enough reason to buy a house?

No.

Or maybe it was if you were a widow with a one-month-old

baby that was super fussy and a toddler who was lonely and bored without her cousins and other kids to play with. I just wanted to get settled somewhere.

It had a lot of great things about it. It was on a cul-de-sac, which made it safer in my mind. It had a huge back yard, which was important to me. A covered back porch for rained-in little kiddos who were dying to get outside. The kitchen and the family room were separated from the rest of the house so our mess could be contained. And I really loved that I could be in the kitchen and basically be in the same room as the kids in the family room. Plus, there was even a cop who lived next door. How safe was that?

But it was boring inside. The walls were painted the-once-fashionable ecru, the carpets were stained with something disgusting, and the house was electric blue.

I could change all that though.

I just needed to believe in myself.

Four days later I called my realtor with a 'yes.' The normal time for negotiations and amendments happened, and it seemed within moments of the acceptance from the seller that my apartment became unbearable.

Joey had been fussy all day and Aubrey was full of energy. *Loud* energy. Get-in-trouble energy.

So I took them to the playground.

Slides.

The slides saved us from the day.

Aubrey loved them.

Once we moved to the new house, I was going to try a housekeeper twice a month. It couldn't be that expensive. My stress level was so high that I couldn't take care of both kids (especially with Joey being so upset all the time), do my errands, go to school, do homework and clean the house.

Even when Rob was alive, he'd have to help out frequently if we wanted to see the floor, or have clean dishes. And Fernanda did all our laundry, too. I couldn't do it all by myself *then*, with just one child.

"Two more slides and then it's time to go home, Aubrey," I called out.

I waved and smiled.

I looked over at Joey in the stroller. He looked like he'd just eaten a purple marker. Or that he had a very smooth five o'clock shadow. I giggled. Thrush medication.

The kids seemed to feel better after our short outing. As I closed the sliding glass door, I remembered that yesterday would have been my parents' 29th wedding anniversary, and my mom had spent her first divorced night in her new apartment. She was here in this complex with me. And now I'd be moving out.

It was funny. I felt overwhelmed and exhausted all the time. I saw no immediate light at the end of the tunnel. I didn't even see it in the not-so-near future. I was losing everywhere. But my mom, she was ecstatic about living alone. Me, not so much.

How different the circumstances were, yet I saw the similarities in our situations, too. We were both starting over. We both lived alone. We could re-invent ourselves. We could try on new things – take classes. We could cry and grieve and be thankful. We could shed old beliefs and make new friends. We could seek companionship and worry about falling into the trap of rebound.

It was kind of nice having someone to go on this journey with me ... even if it was just my mom.

No offense, Mom.

ONE NIGHT, I LIT A CANDLE AFTER PUTTING THE CHILDREN TO BED. I stared in the flame and tried to drown in the flickers.

There must be a fine line between repression and denial, and being okay. Was I done grieving? Was I supposed to move on now? Some days I felt like I could. Most days I didn't.

I could find joy in the bouquet of daisies on my table, I watched romantic movies, I read spiritual books that brought me some peace ... intellectually anyway. *That seems like I'm getting better.* But. I also did a lot of waiting.

I waited – for no one to come home. I waited – for no one to come to bed with me. No one to share funny or endearing stories with. No one to join me in my excitement for my young children's milestones, or in my ongoing quest for God and the spiritual enlightenment.

I mean, yes, my mom – but. It was totally not the same. She didn't live with me. She wasn't there when I drank coffee in the morning. She wasn't there when I looked up from my journal to share something that just clicked for me.

A little sphere of golden light surrounded the candle that I had set on the computer table in the living room. Everything looked different by candlelight. It was softer, slightly askance. Shadowed. Ambient. Fragrant. I wondered ... it might be great to look at life as though seeing it through candlelight. How much more might we understand if we did?

I picked up the candle and centered it in the palm of my hand. All I wanted to know was if I was repressing my pain or if I was really okay right then.

Looking back, what I *really really* wanted to know, was if I could start dating yet. Was it time *for that?* But I didn't want to be the kind of girl who would ask that question. Or maybe I just didn't know *when* I could ask that question and still be a good girl. After all, which widow thinks "Yeah, grieving's a bitch. So when do I get to start dating again?" And I didn't *actually* want to start *dating* dating again. I just didn't want to be alone.

I told myself I wasn't ready to stop feeling the pain because then I would be forgetting – and that must never happen. I wanted and needed companionship, yet I cringed and felt physical disgust at my weakness.

If I grasped at an unsuitable relationship just because it was convenient, like a drowning man groping for a life preserver, I would never forgive myself. It would disrespect Rob's memory, confuse my children and do untold horrors to my psyche.

And so I was afraid to move. Afraid to put my foot out for fear of treading on uncertain ground. Actually, I wasn't so afraid of walking in the wrong direction or making a false step, but of not being able to find my way out of the hole once I was there.

So where do I go? What do I do?

And then I was talking to Rob again.

Do you remember the day I told you I loved you for the first time?

THE FIRST TIME I TOLD ROB I LOVED HIM WAS IN AURORA, COLORADO at the army base we were stationed on. We had been walking around after dark near a baseball field.

"There's something I want to tell you." I had slipped my hand in his and led him to the dugout. We sat down next to each other. "I don't know how to say it." I looked away from him, across the field. It was lit by two watery lights. Enough to feel safe by, but not enough to feel exposed.

"Tell me," he said.

I was silent. I couldn't bear the thought of telling him this prickly, hot, emotional, soaring, painful thing. How could I tell him I loved him? The last man I shared my heart with stomped on it. He had left me broken and unable to find myself among the wreckage for a year.

It was true. I loved Rob desperately. Clawing, brutal, pull your hair out love. I had to tell him. But fear clamped my vocal cords and took my breath so that I whimpered.

Rob put his arm around my waist and curled me into him.

"What is it?" he whispered. "Tell me, *Carida*." He kissed my temple.

I climbed onto his lap and straddled him. I crushed my lips to his and kissed him with passion and fear and giddiness. *I could tell him.*

He pulled away. Concern and acceptance and calm radiated from him.

"Tell me." Insistent.

"I love you!" I blurted it out and then hid my face in his neck. I think I might've cried a little. Tears to release the pent up promises I held near my heart.

"*Carida, Carida.*" He pushed at my shoulders to sit me up but I clung to him, still hiding.

"Hey. *Hey.*" He pushed again harder. I sat up and dared myself to look in his eyes.

"Is that what you were going to tell me?" He smiled. His teeth shown in the shadowed light.

I nodded and looked down, hugging myself.

He laughed.

I looked up. Sharp, with fear crashing on my head once again. Was he laughing at my offering?

"Oh my God," he said and pulled me into a crushing hug. "I thought … I thought …" and he laughed again. He rocked me back and forth. "I thought you were going to tell me something really bad. You were so serious." Now that his own fear was gone, he clucked and chided me like a hen.

"Well, it was hard for me to say," I said, sitting up.

He smiled again and then put it away. He looked me solemnly in the eyes.

"I love you, too."

It was a memory that I took with me always.

How would that ever happen again? How would I ever have the courage to love again? And without love, there was no passion. Without passion, there was no life.

I felt so hypocritical during the daylight hours. I did "Aubrey and Joey" things and ignored the housework piling up and ate gummy bears. But. What I really craved was to sit with a candle in the palm of my hand and to decide if I was repressing or if I was really okay.

If I carried on with whatever life handed me, society would nod its head, approving of the time spent mourning. But I was not a part of that society. At least not today. Not this week, or month. I didn't belong. I didn't know if I wanted to date again. Fernanda never did. Should I? I couldn't bear the thought of being alone, but ... I couldn't bear the thought of being with someone *not Rob*.

And so I sat, holding my candle.

CHAPTER 14

> *Aubrey sleeps the way you did...*
> *~me*

It was a hot August night. I was tired; it was 9:30 p.m. and both kids were still awake. Aubrey, for the moment, was silent. I could hear her bed sheets swishing around as she moved. Occasionally she murmured to herself. Joey was grunting and squirming. He was mad. I wasn't sure what he wanted, but the louder he got, the louder Aubrey got.

We were all settled beautifully in our new home. The first couple of nights were spent on an air mattress in the family room, *camping*, which Aubrey loved. A lot of the painting was done before we moved in. The exterior, too. It was now a light and soft green. The neighbors were ecstatic.

I also had hardwood floors installed in the entry and dining room, and new carpet throughout the rest of the house. The family room carpet was a nice sturdy denim blue shag. The rest an off-white, speckled berber. I thought maybe that was a mistake, but it was gorgeous nevertheless.

Every room was painted a different color. Almost. Aubrey's room, the kitchen and the family room were a lovely pale yellow;

Joey's room was a country blue; mine a serene green – much like the outside color of the house. The center of our home – the sunken living room, dining room and hall – was a dusty rose color that would change hues throughout sun-kissed days.

The living room was the quiet room. No children allowed unless invited. No TV; only quiet activities could be done in there. It was my sanctuary. A matching set of couches, a gorgeous square coffee table, and an Oriental rug all tied it together in the center of the room – conversation pit style. Along the three walls were the fireplace, my great-grandpa's buffet table, and a handmade wooden chest. All of Rob's things that I had kept were in there.

The family room housed our squishy green couch from the apartment, a new desk and filing cabinet (which was big enough to hold Rob's 42 inch TV! – *remember how big those things used to be?*), my computer, and a myriad of baby things that multiplied when I wasn't looking. Like the swing, bouncy seat, and the exer-saucer.

I really did love this house and I felt proud that I could make it this beautiful. It fit me and reflected who I was underneath. I could breathe here. I felt … at home here.

But at what cost? I crawled into my bed for the night and smoothed the duvet down around me. The life insurance money felt like blood money. I used blood money to purchase this house and create a home for Aubrey, Joey and me.

I'd rather be poor and have Rob with us.

The children had fallen silent. I'd planned to watch a movie. It was all set up – candles were lit, I had a drink – but strangely enough, I wasn't interested anymore.

I had looked for love after my divorce. Normal, because I believed – like everyone else – that I was just with the wrong person and that Mr. Right was still out there, waiting to be discovered. And I was right.

I couldn't love the next man any *more* than Rob, and he certainly wouldn't be loved the *same* as Rob. Wouldn't it stand to reason then, that he would be loved *less*? And what good was that to anyone? It would only be convenient.

I felt disgruntled. Angry. Sad. I shoved myself under the covers and yanked the bed sheets to my chin despite the heat..

Perhaps the new man would be loved *differently*, rather than less. The human emotional system was capable of so many facets of love. Surely one woman could love more than one man – *right?* – because she has more than one emotion.

Every time I swallowed my tears down, I felt like I was suppressing myself. I didn't mean swallowing in the pretend hypothetical sense; I actually swallowed in order to stop crying. I didn't want that to make me sick though. It just never seemed to be the right time to cry. Here I was – in bed, by myself, no responsibilities. The children were sleeping. I had time to cry now, *wanted* to, and I knew it would make me feel better, like throwing up makes you feel better.

But nothing.

Dry.

I blew out the candles and went to sleep.

After pottery class one night, a fellow student named Sue ran out to my car – it was actually an SUV now; I traded in the black car that reminded me so much of a hearse.

She had shoulder-length brown hair always tucked behind one ear, and a hard runner's body.

"I heard you talking in class today about what happened. I'm so sorry."

I never knew what to say to other people telling me they were sorry about Rob dying. Even when it was slightly modified, like in *Sense and Sensibility* when Mrs. Jenning's son-in-law says, "I'm more sorry than words can say."

When people said that to me, my first and only thought was: Well, me too. *I'm* sorry he died, too. I'm devastated. Adrift.

People don't know what to say to grieving ones, but we don't either.

Like when I went shopping with my mom during my first visit to Oregon after Rob died. We were at a consignment shop to pick up some maternity clothes for me, because I'd already started showing.

I ran into a girl I'd gone to high school with, also pregnant, also with her mom. She chatted happily about her family and her plans and even mentioned her husband. I plastered a fake smile on, chuckled and said, "Me, too." I left as soon as I could and hoped I never ran into her again.

I couldn't tell her about Rob. It would've terrified her – people think widowhood is somehow contagious. Or perhaps it's just the sudden realization that everyone's mortal and the same thing could happen to them. People don't want a reminder of *that* having lunch with them. Besides, she wouldn't have known what to say, and I hate putting people in that position – where their eyes widen, and fear and sadness and grief pool in them and their mouths open and close like a fish flapping on the shore.

I didn't want to do that to her. It would've ruined her day. So I laughed instead, and waved good-bye.

So. Susan. She was standing in front of me. She was sorry that I suffered this loss.

"Me, too," I answered back.

She nodded her head in acknowledgment.

"I moved here about a year ago to help out my sister and her baby. Her husband wasn't home a lot because of work. You look a bit worn out, like my sister did back then. I bet you're under a lot of stress trying to do everything yourself. I'd like to give you my phone number in case you ever need someone to watch the children for you."

She handed me a slip of paper with her name and number on it. *Wow.* Someone out of the blue like that, just offering help?

"Well, thank you. I'll probably do that." I chuckled. Awkward. I tried to play it off like it was no big deal, but when she went back inside, I treated the slip of paper like the Holy Grail and placed it on my dashboard with reverence.

I went home and told my mom, who had been babysitting for me during my night-time pottery classes at the Benton Center in Corvallis. She agreed that Sue was probably a sane and responsible person and that I should go ahead and give her a try.

I did. I invited her over to talk and we discovered an amazing amount of shared interests and commonalities. I glowed a little brighter in my new friend's presence, and I added to the list one more thing I was grateful for.

My list seemed to be getting longer during those early Oregon days. I saw my massage therapist at least every three weeks and our sessions always began and ended with time spent having tea and talking in his office. Another friend with many shared interests. Writing, among them. I religiously took pottery classes and started feeling the stories inside me come out in the clay. And my neighbors were wonderfully cool.

On one side, I had a family with three teenage girls. Jackpot babysitters! It was a source of much relief to be able to call one of the girls over to play with the kids for a half an hour while I went running.

On the other side of me was the police officer. He came over when I first moved in and offered to do work around my house for me when and if I needed it.

I had him install a peephole and one of those chains for the front door. I was scared a lot then, so anything I did to help me feel physically safe was good. I even had a monitored security system installed.

I had sat on the floor near him when my policeman neighbor had worked on the front door, and I listened to him talk about his divorce. My ears perked up. And then I wondered at myself. Was I maybe starting to be ready to think about dating? I shook it off and went back to listening.

In running, writing, pottery, massage, and monthly-pedicures-just-because, I started to heal.

CHAPTER 15

> *I was looking through our wedding photos and touching your face, glossy beneath my fingertip. I had Aubrey in my arms and I prayed aloud to let God let you know how much we missed you and loved you. Aubrey spread her arms wide and said, "This much!"*
> ~me

One good thing about not having a husband is all the time you have to think – *headsmack* – and something that dawned on me one day was I wasn't sad for *him* having to miss the special family days, like first teeth and dance recitals, I was sad that he wouldn't be there to share those things with *me*. I was sad for *me*.

There were ten more days until the one-year anniversary of his death. On August 17th, 2000, he left this life and began another.

And so did I.

I was in Raynham, Massachusetts that week, visiting family. His family. Our family. Okay, *the* family. I was sleeping in 'our' bed while I was there. The one I left behind when I moved out to Oregon. I hadn't wanted to sleep in the bed we shared when I started over. But here I was, sleeping in our marriage bed again. And I missed him because of it.

I missed the people there, too. I loved Fernanda. She was such a beautiful person.

And I could talk to my friends about Rob there. No one knew him in Oregon. Except my parents, and then they didn't *really* know him. They'd only seen him a handful of times over the years we were together. In Massachusetts I could tell my friends that I just called on him and asked him to come whenever I needed him and he did. So far. I wondered if my welcome with him ever ran out? Would he ever stop showing up in my dreams, or coming to talk with me in my journals despite my asking him to? Would he say, Enough is enough?

In the language of flowers, rosemary stood for remembrance. Fernanda's *house* was rosemary. I recalled things while being in her house that didn't even happen there, but I gobbled them up just the same.

I remembered trying to make love in a hot tub, or the time in our car in an unfinished subdivision, and once in a vacant building on post.

I remembered trying to wake him up in the mornings – I had to set the alarm an hour before he needed to get up and wake him up in fifteen minute increments and then massage his hands and feet and lower legs because he said that it felt like his blood wasn't moving yet, and he couldn't move until it did.

I remembered him locking himself out of our apartment in Denver when he did the laundry in the middle of the night.

The fire in our apartment building.

Smoking the crap cigarettes so we'd want to quit.

Walking in the rain to the lodge on base to rent a room so we'd have some privacy before we were married.

I remembered all our camping trips and when he lost his wedding ring and felt so bad about it that he secretly bought an identical one and only told me about it after he was wearing the new one.

I remembered that famous hug behind the army hospital – the one that always stuck with him for some reason, but to me was just love and safety expressed.

I remembered his protectiveness of me while I was pregnant, of making love after Aubrey was born and having milk leak all over us, of him taking me on surprise drives: Provincetown, the beach, an ice cream store, Burlington Coat Factory for a Christmas present, and local foliage trips to see the leaves turning in late September.

I remembered him telling me stories of his past: which bar he frequented, dealing at the Green in Taunton, and keg parties in the swamps.

I remembered seeing the Red Sox play – we even took Aubrey on that trip – and watching the Boston Bruins with him. That was my first (and only) live hockey game.

I remembered his dreams and fears, and how a lot of them were my own.

I felt alive there in Massachusetts.

Or maybe, I just felt *him* alive there.

THE CHILDREN AND I TRAVELED TO KENTUCKY NEXT, FOR MY SISTER'S wedding. There, I met Leslie's new family. She'd actually already married my brother-in-law. They were doing what Rob and I had done. We got married when we wanted to, and then re-married so that all the family could celebrate with us.

Everyone at the rehearsal dinner was married. I sat on the couch and played with the children while partners in love grouped together and giggled. We watched a video that someone made of Leslie and her fiancé husband. We gathered in the living room and sat on the floor around the coffee table. The song "Rosemary's Granddaughter" played and pictures slid by showing looks of love.

My face felt rubbery and my eyes like lumps of rock. All my

healing and growing that I'd done seemed to drip off and pool around me. It sunk into the carpet.

The one-year anniversary came while I was there and once the sky turned dark, I found a place in Leslie's backyard to sit and write. I lit four candles in a ceremony I hoped to carry on for many more times. I thought Aubrey and I and baby Joey would appreciate it as a sacred ritual to remember Rob.

After that I started writing down all the things I missed about Rob. Yet another list – like I was compulsively trying not to forget him.

I missed him bragging to his co-workers about how I was a great wife. About how I got up in the wee hours of the morning to pack lunches with fat sandwiches and still had sex with him whenever he wanted.

I missed him holding me. I missed him loving me. I hadn't noticed before, but someone showed me – in all the pictures I had of him, he was smiling like every problem or nightmare he'd ever had melted away when I walked in the room.

When I asked him one time what his favorite thing about me was, he said my hugs.

I stopped writing. I couldn't breathe. *It will never be right again.*

How could I find the gift I knew was there? Where was the lesson in all this pain?

I wouldn't give up my life with Rob, my memories. But this emptiness and hollow void couldn't be filled until I met up with him again. I longed for our next life together.

I resumed writing.

I wanted to make him proud. But I felt weak at the same time. I liked the idea of him watching me from some collegiate spirit realm where he studied for exams, readying for another go. I wondered if he could see me, sitting in Leslie's backyard. I wanted that life that we dreamed about. I wanted that big porch and sitting on rocking chairs as we grew older.

I held my breath watching the candles flicker, half-terrified half-hopeful they would blow out.

I wanted to immortalize him somehow, but he was already immortal – in the spirit realm. I wanted to enshrine him, but then how could I move on? I didn't want to move on. Maybe that was the truth of it. It seemed so final, like I could never think of him again if I dated another. And anyway. How would I ever find a man that wanted to date someone with kids?

I wanted to see the clouds rolling by because then I would know the whole world hadn't stopped because I was in anguish. But it was dark out there. Crickets chorused around me. The black Kentucky air was velvet – soft and warm. I watched the candles and the flames that struggled against the breeze.

Three were out. The last flame fought.

One year.

A lone plane engine rolled in the distance. Birds sounded mean, indignant of being roused from sleep. Or was it bats?

The air smelled of barbeque charcoal, grass and dirt and I was overcome with gratitude and thankfulness for the hospitality my sister and her new family had shown me during that visit. A warm light probed from the kitchen onto my journal pages and an orange kitten padded softly across the patio as I tried not to think of bats.

The last candle blew out. The breeze ruffled my hair and caressed me. *Or was it Rob?* I didn't want to go in. I wanted to stay outside in the dark and feel his presence, or hope to. Sometimes I thought he must be too busy to visit, but other times I knew he was there.

I didn't want to face questioning glances tonight. But I had to go in to see if the children needed me, and besides: the candles were out, I couldn't really see the page, and what if those *were* bats?

Please Rob, will you stay with me tonight? I miss you. I miss us. That's the truth.

The crickets sounded like they were fighting.

What if moving towards the next highest and best part of my

life took me away from Rob? What if I shriveled up and never accepted happiness again?

When does the war end?

I love you, Rob. I can't wish you a happy anniversary. Not this year. Maybe next.

MOM AND DAD FLEW HOME THE SAME DAY I DID, ALMOST THE EXACT same time, though on a different flight. Mom offered to take Joey with her, so I only had to keep Aubrey busy.

"Yes, please!" I gushed. "I'm afraid I'd fall asleep while holding him and drop him."

On the flight home, I was exhausted. Even my eyelashes hurt. I tried to write, in an attempt to stay awake, but my head bobbed and my hand flopped on the page making undecipherable marks in my journal.

Aubrey kept bothering the passenger beside us but my attempts at warding her off of him were futile because my eyes keep rolling back in my head. Maybe reading would work better. I managed to detach Aubrey from our neighbor and she promptly began drawing a picture of a bird pooping.

CHAPTER 16

Do you miss me where you are?
~me

Aubrey was about to start pre-school. I'd been longing for some structure to our days – especially with just having gotten back from Massachusetts and Kentucky – and this would be a good start. I needed to settle here. Find my bearings. Being with my family so recently sure made it lonely at our new place with nothing to look forward to. I looked around the family room and tried to tune out *The Wiggles* on Disney Channel. Aubrey was up from her nap and industriously cataloguing her toys she'd missed while she was back East. Joey was still sleeping. The sun shone through the sliding glass door from the back porch.

The house was coming together. My computer was set up; the high chair and swing well used. There was an occasional box huddled in some of the rooms, and the trim in the living room and in my bedroom were still unpainted, but for the most part the house was slowly becoming ours.

I checked on Joey and remembered that the window in his room didn't lock. That freaked me out. I left the door cracked open so I could hear him when he awoke and kind of hovered in the living room and kitchen.

While I waited for Joey to wake up, I recalled the movie I watched the night before. *Bounce.* In it, a father got on the wrong plane at the wrong time and died in a plane crash. The mother forever wondered after that if *any* decision she made was the wrong one. Sending her boys on a bus. Was that the bus that would crash? If she didn't put them on the bus and sent them on foot instead – would they get hit by a car that day?

I found myself wondering things like that, too.

I shook my head. I couldn't think that way though. I'd go insane.

Joey started murmuring and I went to his room. His eyes lit up when he saw me enter. His arms pumped and he rose his feet to the sky in a stretch.

"Hi, little boy." I smiled and cooed and reached for him. I changed his diaper, snuggled him to me and carried him to the kitchen to make a bottle.

After he drank his fill and I set him up in the exer-saucer, I called the neighbor girls to see if any of them wanted to come over for a half an hour so I could go running.

Aubrey galloped to the babysitter when she got there and Joey jumped up and down. I smiled. With my Saucony sneakers laced tightly, I was ready to go and lose myself to the wind. I waved and headed for the door, but Aubrey didn't even look up.

She was so ready for school.

The late summer breeze blew through my hair and cooled my face. My feet padded softly on the pavement. I liked to run alone, if it was safe, and to hear the birds calling out their names. To hear my breath singing its song -- *in, in, out, in, in, out* – in time with my feet.

Rounding the corner back into my cul-de-sac, I jogged to my house. I saw a man sitting on my policeman neighbor's front step, talking on his cell phone. He was young with a shaved head, wearing shorts and a white t-shirt. I smiled and he acknowledged me with a nod. I went inside.

I wonder who that was.

It turned out his name was Rodney. He was a long time friend of my policeman neighbor, and Rodney was staying with him. My neighbor's divorce was final by then and Rodney was moving into the guest room. Bachelors. Cute ones. I thought of all manner of ways to legitimately go over and talk to them. Some worked and some sounded false even to my ears. I was sure they were on to me.

Sue, the woman from my pottery class, had moved in with me in exchange for some childcare here and there, and we'd decided to run a marathon together. We had a running schedule but couldn't run *together* because of the children. Sue watched them most times when I went out running, so Rodney started going with me. We began talking and emailing and phoning each other. He worked ludicrous hours, but we still managed to strike up a friendship. Having him right next door was pure bonus.

Generally, I started the coffee pot at 5:30 a.m. Joey usually woke up around then and I tried to get in a yoga workout before Aubrey got up. Joey was easier to manage while I did yoga. Sometimes Sue did it with me and we'd drink coffee together afterwards. She always drank her coffee in a tall glass instead of a mug. I liked the color that came through the transparent glass. In a mug, you couldn't see it, but I liked handles with my coffee.

One Fall day, after yoga, Sue hit the shower. I poured myself a mug of coffee and transferred Joey from the swing to the high chair. I thought maybe we'd try some rice cereal that morning. If not, at least it was a different location for him to be in. He still couldn't sit up by himself, so he was limited to the floor – which wasn't very safe with Aubrey running around him – his swing, or the exer-saucer. The high chair gave him a different vantage point. He'd like that.

Aubrey wandered out in her pajamas, and I went searching for her Cheerios when the phone rang. It was Mom.

"Turn on the TV." She was breathless.

"Where are you? At work?"

"Not yet. Turn on the TV. Something big is happening. Terrible."

My adrenaline shot up.

"What is it? What? What channel?"

"It doesn't matter. It's on all of them. But I'm watching CNN."

I turned on the TV.

Holy Shit. I was motionless, the remote still in my hand.

"What's happening?"

"They're saying it's not an accident and that someone hijacked the plane," Mom said. "Listen, I have to finish getting ready for work. I'll call you later. I can't believe this is happening."

All day I went back to the television in the bedroom and watched the same footage over and over. There was no new information, but I couldn't help myself. I was drawn back like a junkie. I didn't want the TV on in the family room. I didn't want Aubrey to see the fear, destruction and tears. So I covertly snuck to my bedroom when I thought she was engaged elsewhere.

In the late afternoon I felt so nauseous and headachy that I cut myself off cold turkey. No more TV.

I called the neighbor girls so I could step out for a quick run. Sue wasn't there right then.

The crisp September air shocked my headache away and I tried to run off some of the fogginess. My arms pumped in unison with my legs. Watching the news and seeing the heartache reminded me of *my* loss and seemed to open the wound anew. It wasn't like it happened all over again. I was just reminded that I *had* lost Rob and suffered because of it.

My feet struck the sidewalk cement.

I was mad.

Pissed.

How dare this happen? Even across the country, it affected me. And not just me. Not only did it traumatize the nation, it re-traumatized all of the grieving community everywhere. Even people who thought they were "done" grieving. Like my dad, for instance.

When Rob died, my dad fell apart. My mom told me that when Dad got the news, he went on a drinking binge and holed up in the spare bedroom for two days.

"Why?" I had asked her over the phone. "He didn't even really know Rob."

"He didn't have to."

I imagined her shaking her head.

"*I* think it was his time to grieve. When he was in the war, he didn't have the time to fall apart when all those friends and fellow soldiers died. When you lost Rob, it was, like, permission for him to finally cry. He wasn't really grieving Rob; I think it was *them*." She had sounded apologetic.

It was like that now with the World Trade Center. The only difference for me was I *did* have time to cry over Rob. But then, a year later, I felt like doing it all over again. Crying. And you better believe I was pissed about that. I set my jaw and ran faster.

In all honesty, I was scared, too. Scared about what, I didn't know. I just didn't feel safe anymore. And that pissed me off, too.

I turned the corner and was thankful the rains hadn't come yet. The sidewalk was still dry and raindrops didn't collect on my glasses. Strangely, *that* was what irritated me most about running. Not, you know, the *exercise*, or the sweating and being out of breath. It was the frickin' raindrops on my glasses. You'd think I'd buy a cap, but I always forgot.

The next night I was going out with Rodney to see *Rockstar* and maybe eat something. I guess we fell under the category of "Let's get to know each other, but not date." So it was just a friendly get-together. That night I wrote to Rob.

Rob,

I still hear your voice. I still feel your presence at times.

I told Aubrey I was sad tonight because I missed you and she reminded me to close my eyes and I'd see you. She also said, " … but I'm here. You love me." Such a wise child.

I felt that you released me a little tonight. I know this is ludicrous but it felt that if you were jealous up there, it's no longer a problem. *Even though you've already said go ahead and move on.*

So, thank you. Even though it makes me feel a little sad. As if I'm needing to say good-bye again.

RODNEY AND I DROVE HOME IN HIS RED MUSTANG WITH THE WINDOW open. It was cold outside, but I wanted the fresh air. The stereo blared and we sang as loud as we could against the sounds of the road, the wind, and the music. We had had dinner at *The Ram* in Salem and then saw the late showing of the movie. It was around midnight by the time we started driving home, yet neither of us were ready for the night to end.

"I want to get a drink," I said in-between songs. I still had to talk loud over the sounds of the road. I could feel that my face was flushed and warm from adrenaline and good times. It had been a long time since I'd been out socially.

I knew we said it wasn't a date. But this felt like a date. He was smiling at me like it was a date. We both didn't want the night to end like it was a date. I conceded. This was a real date. My *first* date since Rob died.

Wow.

I purposefully – but with a sigh of nostalgia and a twinge of grief -- pushed any thoughts of Rob aside and looked at the man beside me, driving.

I smiled with pure goofiness. Hormones and happiness flooded through me. He was so handsome. And he laughed. Easily. There was no awkwardness with him. No moments of silence that begged to be broken.

"You wanna go out? Find a bar?" he asked.

I pondered. I needed to get home so that Susan didn't worry if she got up in the middle of the night and found me still gone.

He saw me pause.

"Or, I've got rum at my house. We could grab it and go over to your place. If you feel you need to get home."

Grateful. So awesome that he thought of that. Who would think of that? I smiled and nodded.

"Yes. That sounds rad." The road was dark in front of us, the headlights aiming the only arrow of light.

With our second drink in hand, we settled on my couch in the family room. We sat on opposite ends, with our backs against the arms of couch, our feet tangled up.

"You have unusually high arches," Rodney said. He pointed to my foot with his drink.

"They say that's a sign of royalty," I said.

"Oh, really?" He chuckled.

I took a sip of my drink.

"You wanna watch another movie?" I asked.

He chuckled again.

"Sure."

We decided on *Tombstone*.

I turned down the lights. I felt warm and happy and buzzed.

"Can I snuggle?" I asked.

"Absolutely!" He seemed surprised but delighted.

I finished off my drink and laid down on the couch beside him. I put my head on his chest and he put his arm around me. I closed my eyes and breathed in the scent of him. It felt so good to have arms around me. I thought briefly of Rob, but he was dead and couldn't hold me like this anymore. And I needed this.

The movie held our attention for awhile but soon I was distracted by Rodney's smell. And his hard chest. I moved my hand across his shirt. He looked at me and I looked at his mouth. I bit my bottom lip. His fingers tightened at my back and my breath caught. I looked at his eyes, blue. His heart pounded under my hand and I inclined my chin forward, closer to those lips.

He kissed me.

Slowly.

Lusciously.

I sucked at his bottom lip and wiggled up higher so we weren't straining to reach each other.

He sat up, pulling me to him so that we didn't stop kissing. We kissed faster now – Val Kilmer as "Doc" beside us on the TV. Our tongues touched and probed and explored with soft darts here and there. Our hands followed suit and we breathed heavy between kisses, our hands touching and kneading.

Rodney pulled away.

"Damn." He said it slow and drawn out like honey drizzling onto a piece of toast.He rubbed his face with one hand and held onto me with the other. Still connected. We smiled at each other. I dried my mouth with my hand and looked to the TV. The credits were rolling.

"We didn't finish the movie." I said and grinned.

He laughed.

"Well." He gestured to me, as if implying he preferred what we had done instead. He leaned over and smoothed back my hair and touched my lips with his, softly. One kiss.

"I have to go," he said with apology. "I need to get some sleep before work tomorrow." He stopped. "I mean today."

My heart was full -- of the possibilities and the sense of beginning. I held his hand. I really didn't want him to go. I wanted him to stay longer.

I stood and pulled him up. We walked around to the side of

the couch and he leaned against the arm. I reached up and kissed him again, wrapped my arms around his neck and pressed my body into his. I could feel his arousal.

"Are you sure you want to go home?" I whispered.

His breath was quick and heavy.

"No."

I smiled in the dark and ran my hands down his body to his belt. And then the button on his jeans. And then his zipper. He tilted his hips forward and I slipped his jeans down. He moaned when I touched him and when I kneeled down, he said, "Ah, Jesus."

"Thank you for last night – this whole night," Rodney said at the door.

"I'm sorry I pushed this far," I said, knowing that he had wanted to start slow and be friends only.

"I'm an adult." He pulled me into a hug. I tucked my head under his chin.

"I think I died and went to heaven for a small part of last night," he said and kissed the top of my head. Cliché, but sweet.

"I'm glad you enjoyed it. Now try to get a nap," I said, suddenly afraid for him commuting to work with no sleep. I felt resigned to feeling this way every time someone I cared about drove while they were sleepy. Baggage that I hadn't counted on.

I closed the door on Rodney, a strange echo of my last good-bye to Rob.

I'd crossed a threshold. My heart pounded and I couldn't breathe for a moment. *My first date after Rob.*

I woke a few hours later and stretched in bed, languid, if not refreshed. I played with my hair and grinned in spite of myself. I mustn't read too much into this. He wasn't going to marry me. I'd basically just met him. Sort of. It had been a month.

What did this mean? Were we dating now? It'd been so long since I'd dated anyone, I didn't know how it was done anymore. He said he only wanted to be friends. But, it seemed to me that our actions last night veered away from friend realm. And then I laughed, but clamped my lips together, not wanting to disturb the children. They were awake, I could hear them, but they hadn't actually demanded my attention. Joey was making little murmurs to himself and Aubrey was swishing around in her blankets.

I wasn't threatened at all by last night with Rodney. It was definitely time for me. Rob had been dead for over a year. But what about Rodney? Was it time for him? Was he freaked out by the speed of our connection? Rob and I had connected super fast. Within a week of meeting each other, we had started dating, and within three months, we were married. Speed didn't bother me. Not when you knew it was right.

If Rodney needed to slow down or back up, that was okay with me, though if I was honest I would prefer he didn't. I wanted it to keep moving forward.

I was all for progression.

I still smelled Rodney on my pajamas. I hummed in the back of my throat and stretched my arms to the ceiling, grinning like the Cheshire Cat. *I think I'm okay about this.*

Aubrey padded into my room.

"Hey sweetie baby. How'd you sleep?"

"Good," Aubrey said, and climbed into bed with me. I hugged her and snuggled her to me, loving the warm closeness. Joey murmured and grunted louder.

"Let's go get Joey-Baby," I said. I gave her kisses all over her silky hair and she giggled.

Aubrey settled herself in the rocking chair while I changed Joey's diaper. I put him into clothes right then, too, because he'd peed through his pajamas. The sheet, though, was surprisingly dry.

"Yay! We don't have to change the bedding!" I told Aubrey.

We went in search of food.

I didn't bother trying to connect with Rodney that day at all. We'd just spent, like, ten hours together, he didn't get much sleep, and he had a full shift of work ahead of him. He wouldn't have had time to think of me even if he'd wanted to. But I thought of him. I couldn't help myself. I wondered what his reaction was to our time together. I wondered what he did during the day. He said he didn't have a regular sleep pattern due to his job. I knew he'd sleep sometime tomorrow and then probably be up for the evening. Maybe I'd call him before my pottery class.

I putzed around for the whole day, trying not to think of Rodney.

The next day after Susan got home from her college classes at LBCC, I got ready for mine at the Benton Center. She was going to watch the kids while I was gone. I helped her get Joey's bottle ready; Aubrey had already eaten dinner and was in her jammies. I told Susan what happened with Rodney and that I was going to invite him over that night again after class. She shared her school gossip and whom she'd met so far at school. College suited her. I hoped she'd be able to do it as long as she could. She was forty and enjoying the opportunity to extend her education and to swim in the fascinating world of microbiology. I smiled as I shook up the bottle. *So* not what I was interested in, but it was cool that she loved it.

Outside, I saw Rodney washing his car in the driveway. I waved and unlocked the car. I got in and rolled down the window, then buckled up. My heart fluttered and my hands felt stiff. *What if he's trying to avoid me? Should I ask him over, or wait until he comes to me?* There was nothing wrong with girls making the first move. And he *did* want to be friends. I clenched the steering wheel. I'd invite him over. For just friends stuff.

"Hi," I called out. I motioned him over. "C'mere."

He shut off the water. I waited for him to approach and reached out my hand to take his.

"I'm leaving for my pottery class right now. I'll be back around 10:15pm if you want to come over for that massage I've been promising you. Is that too late for you?"

He laughed, kind of a snort, and shook his head.

"No," he said, "I'll come over."

I squeezed his hand just long enough to let him know I wanted him to come closer. With my right hand resting on the steering wheel, the other traveled up to the back of his neck.

"Can I kiss you?" I asked in a whisper.

His reply was exactly what I wanted.

After class I knocked on his door. My clothes were covered with clay slip and a pencil was stuck behind my right ear. I only just remembered it. At least my hands were clean; I'd washed up before I left the studio.

"Hi," I said when he opened the door. "I'm home now. Gimme a few minutes to change my clothes and I'll be ready for you."

At home, I agonized over what would be semi-flattering to wear. I still had Joey's baby fat on me and while I was losing weight every day, most of the more flattering clothes were not quite as flattering as I liked yet. I only had a minute or two to agonize though, so I just pulled off the dusty clothes and put on a pair of denim shorts and a clean t-shirt. My legs were shaved and my toes were painted red. Good enough.

I checked on the babies and saw that Susan was reading in her room. A strip of light shone under her door. I scratched on it and whispered, "I'm home. Rodney's coming over. I'm giving him a massage."

"Okay. Good night, Valerie."

I turned on the computer in the family room and put a soothing CD into the tray. I didn't have candles, but the screen saver was awesome, so I used that as ambiance. Also the dining room light was on in the background.

Rodney knocked on the door quietly. I ran and opened it. A little giddy, I invited him in. I tried to pull off the it's-cool-I'm-just-giving-a-therapeutic-massage-here (just as friends, of course), but I didn't know if I was successful.

"I don't have a massage table, or anything, but I laid out a couple of blankets for padding here on the family room floor for you."

"It's great. It's fine. I just really need the massage, you know?"

"Sure." I gestured him to the floor. I hoped the kids wouldn't wake up.

He lay down on his belly, then remembered his shirt, lifted himself up cobra pose-style and pulled it off over his head. He sunk back into the floor and turned his face to the side. I slathered some lotion on, straddled his lower back, and started working on his shoulders and neck.

After fifteen minutes, or so, I moved myself so that I was sitting beside him. I worked on his lower back.

"Do you want me to massage your hips?" I compressed my fist through his track pants.

"Yeah," he said. His voice was muffled and he cleared his throat. He was drowsy and slow. Relaxed. He put his forehead on the floor and arched his back like a cat. He slipped his pants and briefs down and exposed his lovely ass. I wasn't expecting that and I bit my lips to keep the sigh from escaping.

Just friends, just friends, I chanted to myself.

CHAPTER 17

"I brought you something." Rodney was at my front door holding a case of Diet Pepsi in his arms. I laughed.

"What's this for?" I asked.

"For me."

"I thought you said it was for me." I smiled.

He wiggled his head and laughed, then walked past me into the house. He headed for the refrigerator, and started sliding cans onto the bottom rack.

"It's so I don't feel guilty for drinking all of yours," he said. "This way I can drink as much as I want." He smiled a little boy smile.

FOR THREE MONTHS, RODNEY CAME OVER AND FED JOEY IN THE HIGH chair, put Aubrey to bed by drowsily tracing his finger over her nose, forehead and cheeks – a sensation she loves to this day – and talked music, philosophy, and personal growth with me. We laughed and went out to dinner, jogged together, and played around back and forth between "just friends" and something more. Despite the fun we had, most of it was a mess of confusion, yearning and denial.

The biggest hurt for me wasn't in the snuggling, kissing and sleeping over. Or that he labeled us "just friends" while we did it. It was the regular everyday stuff. Rodney hanging out in his pajamas watching football with me, or playing with the kids.

I wanted romance from my next partner, but not of the storybook variety. I wanted real-life romance. Holding hands, a shared private joke, watching TV, taking the kids to the zoo.

What hurt was that Rodney and I *did* most of that – despite our "friendly" status. It hurt because my heart remembered doing all those things within the parameters of a romantic relationship. Doing those things with Rodney confused my heart and mind. My heart said it meant one thing and my mind said it was something else. Or rather *Rodney's* mind said it was something else.

Snuggling, and what that lead to for us -- whether sex happened or not – needed to stop. I *wanted* something to happen – but not for pretend. This felt like a real romantic relationship to me. So, if he didn't want to be my boyfriend, then our behavior around each other had to change. For my heart's sake. I couldn't continue pretending that he felt other than he did.

Sitting in the hot tub one night (a luxury I conceded to when I was "adding character" to the house), I explained this to Rodney. I sat on the other side, far away from him. He apologized profusely. He didn't ever want to hurt me. He was being selfish. It was all his fault. When I tried to take ownership of my actions and behavior towards him, he shushed me away with an attempt at chivalry.

And then silence from both of us. The water jets bubbled and my fingers got plump and wrinkled. Rodney cleared his throat.

"I guess this means you aren't coming to Eugene with me tomorrow?"

Oh yes, our trip. I sighed. Rodney was contemplating attending U of O for a nursing program and wanted to tour the campus. He'd asked me along last month. We were going to stay in a hotel and be up early for the guided tour, getting home midday so he could sleep before his night shift. I really wanted to go. Just for the break in monotony. I already had childcare set up. Mom was going to stay with them overnight, and drop them off at their in-home daycare place the next day.

"Well."

And with that, I was going. We re-set our boundaries and what that would look like in our daily interactions, and we went to Eugene with platonic hearts. We found our hotel, we ate dinner, we watched a movie at the theater, we went to a bar and had a couple of drinks and played pool. All platonically.

And then we went to our hotel room.

With two beds.

"I wish you liked me more," I said. The bathroom light was on, leaving his face in shadows. We stood in between the two queen-sized beds.

He clucked sympathy and his hands swallowed my face, tenderly pulling me to him.

"I like you *too* much. If I didn't like you as much as I do, I'd have sex with you, no problem."

Somehow through alcohol and desire, that didn't end up being contradictory to him un-dressing me, and me finding his lips.

WE TRIED *REAL* DATING FOR TWO WEEKS AFTER THAT EUGENE TRIP. The kind of real dating that meant I got to call him my boyfriend. But it just didn't work.

When we did end, on a drizzly day in November, our friendship managed to continue and we both began dating other people.

I grew a lot with Rodney, and I thanked him for that. Because of him, I knew what I wanted, I knew how to be safe with someone, and he helped me continue to laugh at myself and stay silly.

I'd wondered why Rodney and I met, if it wasn't because we were supposed to partner together. Being with him was great. I really liked him. And *every time* I was with him I liked him more and more. He just didn't want the same things I did out of our relationship. And in order to maintain our friendship, I had had to set boundaries. *Maybe that's why I met him.* To learn how to set boundaries for myself.

In retrospect, I know why it all happened. Not in a cosmic-meant-to-be sort of way, but just practically. Rodney was lonely, as was I, and we needed the skin. We needed to feel needed. We needed the companionship of someone. Neither of us were ready for a long term commitment, and that's why it didn't work. Rodney knew we were meant for only friendship, so sex felt bad for him – knowing he was hurting me emotionally every time he succumbed.

One night on the couch he pleaded for an answer, "Why do I feel so drawn to you?" At the time, I thought it was because he loved me, but was fighting it. But really it was for the companionship and nurturing. We both needed it. At least, that's my take on it. Rodney might very well have a different idea on why we came together and didn't last.

"What do you want?" Susan asked me one day. We were in the living room finally painting trim. Well, Susan was. I was watching. She was on a ladder with a little brush in her hand, dabbing up near the ceiling.

"I want to feel loved and cherished. I want someone to hold me when I feel broken and lost. I just want someone to love me. I miss that."

Susan nodded. I was angry and shoved my hands in my jeans pockets. I twisted my toes into the carpet and contorted the muscles in my face.

"I never wondered if Rob loved me, you know?" I looked down at the floor and felt my face soften. "He let me know in so many ways. Not only did he say it a gazillion times a day, he showed it in everything he did."

Susan continued dabbing, understanding somehow, I guessed, that I needed to vent.

"He'd pick a flower for me, or call me at work, or *from* work if I was at home. He'd clean the kitchen or take me on a surprise drive, or take me out to dinner, or play with Aubrey on the floor so I could just sit for a bit. How do I replace that?" I looked up to Susan.

"Maybe you don't," she said.

"So what do I do now? I'm ready to let someone else in my heart." I flopped on the couch. "I'm not the sit-idly-by-and-wait-for-something-to-happen kind of person. Yet, going on a hunt for a man seems so unnatural. Forced." I grimaced. *"Loser."*

Susan shook her head and loaded up her brush from the paint can.

"No. Not a loser. You're a mom with a *baby*. You can't meet guys in the usual fashion. Try *match.com* or something."

I made a face.

"Well, it's less unnatural than you going to a club when you've got a baby at home. That's not you. This way you can look for exactly what you want and you have more control."

"Maybe," I said. Melancholy. Distrustful.

"Mommy! Mommy!" Aubrey ran up to the room but not into it. Her three-year-old face shone with euphoria. She was holding a mylar balloon in the shape of a cluster of fish left over from her birthday party. She sped back and forth behind the couch with the fish trailing behind her.

"Mommy, Mommy! I caught a fish! I caught a fish!"

Her eyes glowed, and love and excitement came off her skin in powerful waves. I laughed and her eyes crinkled and she giggled with little teeth showing. I opened my arms and she ran in for a hug. I was so thankful and blessed to have this little creature entrusted to me. I no longer felt despondent and I left Susan to the painting while I got ready for another pottery class.

I had several cups to glaze and then they'd be ready to high fire. Pottery was both fun and cathartic for me. A creative outlet, anyway. Pottery had enabled me to understand things about myself that I didn't know or weren't fully formed in my mind before. Many things, actually.

Pottery reminded me that there was art everywhere I looked. From the frozen dew drops on a tree branch, to the way a line crackled through the sidewalk. From the color of Joey's eyes, to the way Aubrey ran when she was happy, to the sound of a lover's breath in my ear when he was excited.

Strangely enough, pottery had shown me that it didn't matter what people thought of me, my actions, or my values. It only mattered what *I* thought, and whether I was showing integrity to my true self. That epiphany arose from my discovery that my favorite pots, mugs or bowls weren't the prettiest.

I was at the pottery studio at the Benton Center in Corvallis sitting with my class on the last day of the term. My instructor had some of our finished work on the table in front of him. Students were gathered around the table, but I sat off a little – at a kick wheel, not the electric ones – and eyed the creations that looked so much prettier than mine.

The instructor wanted to know what we'd learned overall from our experience in the class. And which pieces we had the most fun making. A pretty standard question, and with it he received fairly standard answers. His eyes stayed focused on the teapots, mugs, and plates. His arms were crossed in front of him.

When it was my turn to speak – I think I waited until the very end – I drew a breath and wondered what to say that hadn't already been said, and still be true.

"My favorites are the ones that feel good in my hands when I close my eyes. If the piece tells my hands a story, then it holds value for me," I said.

The instructor looked up straight into my eyes, and held them. He smiled and nodded his head. My roommate, Susan, later said that I was the only one of us that got a smile.

It was sad that most people wouldn't agree with me on the

pottery thing. Society would hold value in the pieces that weren't lopsided or had fingerprints in them.

It used to be, once upon a time, that I would agree with mainstream notions on any point in order to avoid confrontation, being singled out, or from my fear of being judged unworthy. But after Rob's death and my growth through my grief, I'd come to realize that in order to live authentically, to truly enjoy myself as a person, I had to ignore society's values and create my own. And to truly *know* that it was okay to have different beliefs than someone else.

It was okay to believe in reincarnation. It was okay to like the lopsided pots better than the straight ones. It was okay to dance in the rain with your toddler. It was okay to cry at a movie that nudged your soul awake. It was okay to have sex when you'd only been widowed for a year and you had small children – and it was okay to be afraid.

Even though society didn't agree.

Or, at least the part of society that lived in Massachusetts about an hour south of Boston.

CHAPTER 18

I read something beautiful once about how people come and go within our lifetimes and why. It was just an internet meme, but it had always stuck with me. Rob was someone I needed to know in this life. I learned from him, and I grew from the pain I endured after his death. The gift – remember the good you can always find in the bad? – the gift that came from Rob's death was my voice. My courage. My strength of character.

I no longer went along with belief structures and ways of life *just because everyone else did them.* And I knew how to do things on my own now. I could buy a house, hire contractors, decide whether or not to circumcise my son, and choose which schools to put my children in. All by myself.

One morning I found out why *Aubrey* was in my life. I was straightening the kitchen and collecting trash from around the house to take out to the curbside. It was drizzling and yucky outside. Thanksgiving and Christmas had come and gone and the New Year had started. But a new year of what?

Joey was too big for the exer-saucer by that time and got into all sorts of things. Thankfully he seemed to be involved in his toys and the TV for the moment while Aubrey "helped" me, which was code for: making everything take longer than it really needed to.

"Stay there," I said, as I hauled the two big white garbage bags to the trash bin. She hovered at the opening to the driveway. I walked quickly through the drizzle, dumped the trash and pulled the bin to the curb. When I turned around, Aubrey was in the driveway, jumping up and down. I shooed her inside with cooing words.

"Get inside, silly. It's wet out here." I smiled a pretend mommy smile that meant *I* didn't want to get wet and wanted to be inside.

"Mommy! Let's dance in the rain!"

I stopped. Instantly put in my place. Of course we should dance in the rain! I was astonished at her awareness of the beauty in all things and her exuberance for life. I took her little hands and we twirled and sashayed and laughed and became breathless.

And that was when I knew why Aubrey came into my life.

To remind me
    To look for magic,
    To remember
    To live spiritually,
    To experience
    Joy
    In dancing
    In the rain.

This wasn't the only time I was stopped in awe for Aubrey's place in my world. On another occasion, ripe with the mundane, I was collecting the Sunday paper from the front porch. It was chilly outside and I wanted to close the door against it and crawl back to my complacent cocoon.

Aubrey pushed out the door past me and gasped.

"Oh Mommy! Let's sit on the step and smell the blue sky!"

It was all I could do to stop from gasping myself. How was this three-year-old so wise and I was so broken and crotchety?

I hugged her with delight, emotion billowing up like flour dust when you add too much too quickly to the bowl, and tried not to let her see the tears starting in my eyes.

MATCH.COM WAS A PLAY-THING. A WASTE OF TIME. AND I STARTED questioning my ... fuckability. Was I a good catch anymore? Would anybody want me? I still had the baby fat from my last pregnancy, and I had two itty bitty kids. Who would willingly walk into that? And plus, was I even *ready* to share the decision-making about parenting? I didn't answer to anyone then – sometimes I quite liked that, other times not so much.

Or, *gag*, if I welcomed someone in my life again, would my quiet room turn into a display room for his model cars? Or posters from my suitor's high school band competition? And then there was always my friends' and family's reaction. Dating someone from the *internet* was still weird and creepy back then.

I went on a series of blind dates and never saw the men again. One time I wrote to a man for a month before we met each other. Again. One time. Never saw him again. What was wrong with me?

Another time I dated someone for two months before he dumped me *by mail*.

And then it was Valentine's Day.

The children were in bed and quiet. The house was dark and I didn't even have the heart to write in my journal that night. I crawled under my covers, defeated. I soberly closed my eyes to the unromantic and helpless day I just spent without Rob, when Aubrey crept into my room hours past when I thought she'd been asleep.

"What's wrong, Aubrey?" I rolled over to face her and brushed back her dark bangs.

"Where's Daddy?"

Quite frankly, this stumped me a little. This wasn't a new question, but it was one I thought we'd dealt with.

"He's in heaven, Sweetie," I said. Aubrey looked down at her hands picking at the blanket on my bed.

"When's he coming home?" she asked.

My heart stopped. Right then. Right up in my throat. I think I can say, that apart from the soldier handing me the American flag at Rob's military funeral, that *that* was the worst moment I'd experienced since Rob died.

"Oh honey," I said, pulling her into my bed and arms. "He's not coming home."

Blam.

My body crumpled at the base of a brick wall.

Somehow I got her back into her own bed and then I cried myself to sleep. On Valentine's Day – when every other lover was having dinner with their sweetheart, eating chocolate and pressing flowers into each other's hands.

And then.

Two days later.

My email inbox had this:

Hi.

I just read your profile and was impressed enough that I had to write. I graduated from Hunter College in New York with a film production degree and a minor in creative writing. The plan was to write and direct my own movies. I gave that up to support a family but am still currently working on a novel in my spare time. I've been working on it for about two years now and am already on chapter four! Okay, so I don't have a lot of spare time.

Anyway, I too would love to find that someone special to enjoy doing every day things with. I've been divorced for about five or six years now and feel like it'd be nice to have someone to share my days and night with.

This is starting to feel a little bit long for an introductory letter so I'll try to wind it up here. Anyway, I'd love to hear back from you. You DO have an amazing smile after all! And, it does seem that we do like doing some of the same things. Hopefully we could enjoy doing some of them together. Of course, the only way to know for sure is for you to write me back.

I hope to hear from you soon,
Paul

HMM. I CLICKED OVER TO MATCH.COM AND LOOKED OVER HIS PROFILE. Nice smile. Loved his hair. But *eek!* He was so tall. I wondered why I found his height so psychologically intimidating. I imagined him looking down on me and that just didn't do at all. I wanted to know that I was on the same level emotionally, intellectually and mentally. But, I shrugged, I should answer him back. He was friendly and he sounded interesting, despite his height. I really liked that he was a writer. Very cool. I acknowledged that my insecurities existed, but decided not to worry about them at that point. His profile said he had a daughter and he loved kids. So he was a dad already and he wouldn't be scared off by my children. *Bonus.*

I thought about it for a day or two and then responded.

The very same day, he wrote back and talked about his novel and a cool story he heard on NPR about Native American Storytelling and then asked a bunch of questions about me, and invited me to email him directly.

Hmm.

And then mommy duties called and I couldn't think about him for awhile.

IT WAS TIME TO MOVE JOEY OUT OF MY ROOM. I WANTED MORE privacy. Rob and Aubrey and I all shared a room for two years. The twenty-two months that she and Rob were both alive at the same time, and then another few months after that, until it wasn't safe for Aubrey to stay in the crib anymore. Sharing a room with Aubrey was necessary then, due to a lack of space. Here, Joey had his own room (though Susan was using it) and Aubrey's room was plenty big to share. And now that I was starting to date more … I didn't think I wanted a lightly sleeping infant sharing space with me.

I only hoped that Aubrey didn't wake up Joey when I put her to bed at night. She got up a lot after I tucked her in, and she sang to herself. But maybe with her brother in her room, she wouldn't feel alone and compelled to leave her bed. Of course, maybe Joey would be the one to wake Aubrey in the night when he cried for food.

Nah.

Aubrey slept like a stone.

I began with re-arranging Aubrey's room to accommodate Joey's crib. Her cheerful yellow walls and wallpaper fairies smiled and fluttered around us. Aubrey was very interested in the change in her room and having her brother in the same room with her every night! Well. It was just too much to be wished for. She was positively vibrating. I vacuumed under where the dresser used to be.

"Now, when Joey is napping, you won't be able to come in here. He'll need quiet to sleep."

"I know, Mommy. I can play with my toys in the family room."

"Yes, baby. That's a good idea." I smoothed her cheek.

I moved Joey's dresser into his new room and nestled it next to Aubrey's.

Dismantling Joey's crib was another thing all together. I had hoped that it would fit through the doorway and I could just push it down the hall. It even had wheels on the bottom. But no. A screwdriver was needed.

Susan helped and we soon finished the task. Rodney arrived then, and he and I went for a run while Susan stayed with the children.

When I got back, there was another email from Paul. I smiled a little at this friendly, creative pen pal I'd stumbled across. But my breath caught when I read his last sentences.

> I don't know about you, but I'm feeling ready to talk on the phone. Call me tonight if you want. I'd love to have a voice to go with the pictures.

"Susan!" I turned from the computer. She was reading the paper on the couch in the family room. "He wants me to call him." My heart started to race a little.

"Then call him."

"What should I say? What if I can't think of anything to say and there's all these weird long pauses?" My voice kicked higher.

She put down the paper and laughed at me.

"I don't know," she said. "Just call him." She picked up the paper again and crossed her legs. The light outside was starting to fade and she was just about to go for a run herself. She had her sneakers on. She finished reading and put the newspaper away. She stretched and chuckled.

"Just call him." She shrugged her shoulders as she headed for the door. "If you want to."

"Ahh!" I called after her. I had plenty of time to agonize, because he didn't want me to call him until he got home from work late that night. After dinner with Susan and the kids, I'd watch a movie to take my mind off it and then I'd just do it. Done. Then I wouldn't worry about it anymore. I'd just do it.

I did, and we talked for *three hours*.

We talked about college (he went, I didn't, and I felt a little stupid talking to him, afraid he'd think I was dumb.)

"No. Don't feel that way. Look, there are probably lots of things that you are more intelligent about than I am. And there are some things that I know about that you don't. You know all about pottery, I know nothing about that. I know about sales; I'm a great salesman. Probably you don't know as much about sales as I do," Paul said.

We talked about his family and mine, we talked about his father not being around (his mother raised him by herself, with the help of a friend), we talked about clothes.

"What's the sexiest kind of clothes to you?" I asked at one point. I was much more comfortable by then. We'd been talking for more than an hour and I was stretched out on the family room couch in the dark. Susan was in her room and the children were asleep.

"Sweatpants."

I laughed.

He laughed.

"No, I'm serious. Sort of. I like stretchy comfortable clothes on a woman. It makes for easy access, and I *know* that when I'm looking at her, and ... it's sexy." I could hear the smile in his voice.

His voice.

I really liked his voice. A sweet combination of rumbly sexy and happy upbeat. He liked to laugh, too. And after the first agonizing ten minutes, or so, he was really easy to talk to.

We also talked about Rob.

"If we ever spend any time together, you'll see that Rob is still very much a part of our lives. We have pictures of him on the walls, we visit his family as often as we can, we even lit a candle on his birthday and sang to him," I said.

"Valerie. I know going into this that you have a past. I have a past. I know I'm not the first guy to ever date you. Of course you have a past."

And strangely, even though the words were far from eloquent,

I was relieved. I hadn't even met this man face to face yet, but I already knew that I really liked him and I couldn't wait for our date that we'd scheduled for Saturday. I wasn't anxious about Paul being uncomfortable with the subject of Rob. It'd be okay for me and the kids to continue to have Rob in our lives and that we wouldn't have to tip-toe around the subject of him when we were with Paul. My breath steadied and I sank further into the couch.

> Friday, February 22nd
> Paul,
> Just got off the phone with you and thought of something funny. I've been wondering what to wear on Saturday (it's a girl thing, bear with me), and it suddenly hit me. I'll wear sweats! LOL
> Just kidding ...
> See ya tomorrow night,
> Valerie

> Saturday, February 23
> Valerie,
> Only do that if you want to drive me wild with desire! Believe me, trying to figure out what you're going to wear isn't just a "girl thing." I spent a decent amount of time this morning trying to pick out something that was also work appropriate. Anyway, in case you're wondering, my daughter Aniela says I did fine.
> Looking forward to tonight,
> Paul

CHAPTER 19

I finally decided on an outfit. Ironically it was one that Paul had already seen, because I had a picture of me wearing it to my dad's wedding on my *Match.com* profile page. I pulled on the fat-schmooshing kind of nylons with spandex in them to make me look better in the skirt. It was a coral color with a subtle monochromatic floral pattern in it. The sweater was the same coral and had a v-neck. I put on some strappy high-heeled sandals and spent just enough time on my hair and make-up. Nothing overdone, but there all the same. My nails were trimmed short with no polish and my toenails peering up through the open-toed sandals were painted red. Of course. There could be no other toenail color.

I kissed Aubrey and Joey good-bye and left them with Susan. I settled myself in my Explorer, careful not to get the back of my skirt too wrinkly. I had the heat on just a little and the window cracked. I didn't want to get all sweaty before I saw Paul. I turned on a Sublime CD and headed to Corvallis. Sublime was usually the band that I listened to when I was angry, but for some reason it called to me that night, and only fed my bounciness. And I actually did a little. Bounce in my seat as I drove. *Car seat dancing.* I laughed out loud when a picture of Aubrey dancing in her car seat came to mind.

Paul worked in Junction City, and with me in Albany, Corvallis seemed a logical place to meet. We were having dinner at a place on the river called, suggestively, Big River Restaurant. Among other things, they served Italian food – one of Paul's favorites. Part of the reason I chose the place.

I WASN'T TOO FAMILIAR WITH CORVALLIS. I CAME HERE FOR POTTERY class, and my massage therapist had an office here. I loved their bookstore, *Grass Roots*, too, but other than that, the way I found things was by driving around until I saw them. Not something I recommended at night.

But I'd done my homework and gotten directions to the restaurant ahead of time, so I confidently pulled into the parking lot and turned off the engine. It looked busy. We didn't have a reservation. A little bit of alarm twinged through my knees, but I recognized that we'd eat there or we wouldn't. And I didn't mind waiting for a table anyway.

I took off my seatbelt and checked my lipstick. *Do I have any lipstick on my teeth?* I smiled in the rearview mirror. *Nope.* I popped in a peppermint Altoid and reapplied some lip gloss over the lipstick. Shiny, slippery lips were actually less of a distraction when I was talking than sticky lipstick. I didn't want to sound funny while I talked. I checked my sweater to see if it was wet under the arms. *Not noticeable.*

I took a few slow calming yoga breaths – hard to do when you were sitting up. It felt like I'd just been kicked in the stomach. I needed to relax.

Should I listen to some soothing music? Why did I listen to Sublime on the way here? I checked my watch. No time to waste sitting around too much longer. I'd come early, but still. I didn't want Paul to arrive and see me sitting in my car. I cleared my throat, put the Altoids in my purse, gathered my keys and got out. I smoothed my skirt, checked my panties – *no wedgie* – and smiled in the darkness to no one.

Inside, I glanced around the waiting area and looked down the bar. No one that looked like it might be Paul. I went back to the hostess to find out how much time of a wait there was.

An hour?!

I quickly added my name to the list. I hadn't planned to. I was going to just wait for Paul to get here first, in case he didn't want to wait for a table. But, it was a Saturday night. Probably everywhere else would be packed, too. I nestled myself on a leather-ish looking couch in the waiting area and wondered briefly why I didn't bring a book with me.

Because you aren't going to read, you're going to talk with Paul. Who brings a book on a date? I asked myself.

At each opened door, I looked up and saw that it wasn't him yet. Ten minutes passed and then the door opened and I knew him right away. He was wearing black slacks, a purple long-sleeved button down shirt and a tie. He had a long black leather coat on, too. With a hood. I loved it. I recognized his black wire glasses from his pictures. And he was tall. Tall. *Did I say tall?* I wouldn't have known by looking at him, but his profile said he's 6'5". *So that's what 6'5" looks like.*

When he saw me, he smiled so big that his face changed shape. I stood up and held out my hand to him.

"Paul." I smiled, too, and felt silly and awkward and happy.

He reached for my hand and enveloped mine with both his own. Like he was *doubly* happy to meet me. It was charming.

I told him about the wait and he didn't mind. He suggested taking a walk. I imagined us like in a movie walking the streets of a city with hands in our pockets. It was romantic and I was momentarily stunned by his offer – feeling at once unworthy and lucky to have been asked.

And then he looks down at my shoes.

"Or maybe you'd rather not. Your shoes."

"No, I'm fine. It's fine. I'd love to walk."

I put on my jacket and he lead me outside. We walked under the street lamps and store fronts of downtown Corvallis. There was construction on the river side, so we couldn't get too close to the water. We talked about nothing and everything, again, like we did on the phone.

We headed back soon though, both of us not wanting to lose the table to the line of patrons behind us on the list. We got a drink at the bar and waited there. When it was time to be seated, the waiter lead us upstairs. I was glad because it seemed a more intimate part of the restaurant, but I wondered what my ass looked like in my skirt to Paul as I was walking up the stairs in front of him. I hoped it looked good. Now that I was consciously aware of my ass, I purposely tried not to swish it extra much and kept my ascent steady and not jiggly.

We sat.

Across from one another.

I drank water as soon as it was poured.

We both ordered ravioli.

And ate lots of bread.

And talked.

And talked.

And talked.

And talked.

It was lovely.

Our meal slowly disappeared and I even ordered dessert to prolong my time with Paul. Finally it was obvious that we were both done and there was nothing to do but leave. He paid the bill. Fine by me. I let him. The dishes had been cleared. Our water was gone. I offered him a mint. We chewed and sucked on our mints and smiled at each other. I giggled.

"I'm having a really good time. I don't actually want this night to be over yet," I said.

Paul smiled. He reached for my hand, but pulled back at the last second and put them through his hair, and then in his lap.

"Is there a movie you want to see?" he asked.

I grinned.

"Actually." I suppressed a chuckle. "There is a movie I've been interested in. *A Beautiful Mind*?"

"Sure. I've heard of that. I'd like to see it. Where's the movie theater?"

Somehow we found it in the dark and drove by to see what time the movie started. We ended up having about forty-five minutes to kill.

"So now what? What should we do while we wait?" I asked.

Paul looked around him, as if he would see something through the windshield in the dark parking lot that would inspire him.

"Is there a book store around here?"

I *really* adored this man. Another lip-stretching smile from me.

"Yes. My favorite one is closed already, but there's a Borders not to far from here." And we again drove around until we found it.

I loved bookstores. They were one of my very favorite places to be. I loved books. I loved all the *potential* in bookstores. All the stories hidden between the book jackets. So many things to learn, so much entertainment. I learned about myself when I read novels, and I grew when I read non-fiction.

I meandered around and smelled the newness of the books, and soon lost myself in my element. I didn't even know where Paul was. He found me and took me back to the music section of the store and put headphones on my ears. I heard Angelique Kidjo for the first time.

We listened to music and talked about books and then it was time to go.

There was a line forming at the box office. Surprisingly. Or maybe not. I'd never actually gone to the movies in Corvallis before. Maybe it was normal.

It was a little chilly and I shivered. My jacket wasn't really a jacket. It was light-weight and more of a long-sleeved shirt.

"Cold?" Paul opened his large coat and invited me in.

Delighted, I sank into the warmth of his body heat and he wrapped his arms and coat around me.

I so loved that.

We hobbled forward in line, still attached by his coat, until the tickets were purchased and we could go inside.

A Beautiful Mind was an awesome movie. Wicked interesting and full of emotions. I cried in parts of it and didn't care that I did so in front of Paul. In fact, I thought he might've cried a little in parts of it, too. We were good together. And that felt hopeful, euphoric, nurturing, and safe. I held his hand in the theater.

AFTERWARDS, HE DROVE ME BACK TO THE RESTAURANT. HE PULLED UP right next to my parking space and parked. He even pulled the keys out of the ignition. *Was he going to get out and open my door? Would he kiss me goodnight?*

Uh. Neither. He just stared at me. And we smiled at each other.

I totally wanted him to kiss me.

CHAPTER 20

Strangely enough, I remembered a phone conversation I had had yesterday with my first husband, Eric, about kissing on a first date. I'd called him to ask for dating advice and he had explained the precise way to stand and tilt your head, and where to direct your eyes, if you wanted a kiss good-night at the end of a date. I had laughed over the information – and also that I had been having that conversation with an *ex-husband* – and felt glad that we had the kind of relationship where we could talk about that sort of thing.

But none of his advice was applicable right then! Paul wasn't leaning over. We were too far away from each other in the bucket seats. I couldn't lean into him. I couldn't look up at him (for once we were eye to eye). I sighed internally, not in a way that he could hear. I was just going to have to do this, wasn't I? I was going to have to instigate and probably make myself look foolish and I'd feel awkward and forward.

But that was probably what guys felt like all the time right before they kissed someone.

So I did it.

I leaned over the console.

I twisted my head to face him as best I could.

And I touched my lips to his.

Eric had told me to kiss lightly at first, like a test kiss, and to pull away just a little before going in for the real kiss. So I did. I pressed my lips into his warmness and then pulled an inch away, asking with my body if he wanted to continue. He retreated and I was a little disappointed. I didn't move anywhere. I hovered over the console in my weird, twisted posture. He quickly leaned back in.

The kiss was hurried and wet and awkward, but somehow nice.

We both pulled back, more than a little embarrassed, I thought. We grinned stupidly and said we'd had a great time and I got out of the car, sliding off the leather seat.

I waved from outside the car and he waited until I drove away before he pulled out of his parking spot. I was giddy on the drive back home. The next day I called my mom and talked about Paul for an hour.

> Sunday, February 24, 2002
> Hi,
> I made it home fine last night. I had my radar detector working overtime and got home at 1:50 a.m. As I was driving home I was bouncing around the FM dial and I found an old radio show with Bing Crosby, Bob Hope and Dorothy Lamour called "The Road to Los Angeles," so even my drive home was enjoyable.
> Paul

> Sunday, February 24, 2002
> Dear Paul,
> I had a *fabulous* time last night. I hope you enjoyed yourself as much as I did. I'm very impressed, if I may be so bold, and am looking

forward to our next date on Friday. In fact, if you want to get together before our Friday excursion, it wouldn't hurt my feelings at all. When you get home tonight, if you want, why don't you give me a call and let me know what you think.

Sunday night I looked outside the sliding glass door in the family room, the phone nestled between my shoulder and my ear. It was dark and raining. I remembered Paul's hands holding mine and that his smile made his pupils do this opening thing, and that when they did that, I was drawn into them.

"I wish you were here right now," I blurted, and then I scrunched my eyes together at how desperate it sounded. But, amazingly, he didn't seem to mind.

"Mmmmm," he said. It sounded like he was purring. "Me, too."

I wanted this man to be here all the time and I wasn't surprised at how fast the infatuation had bulldozed over me. Now, while I didn't think I'd marry Paul within the next three months – there were some similarities to the speed at which my relationship with Paul was taking off.

Okay, okay. We'd only technically been on one real date, *but* we'd talked on the phone at least four times, for long periods of time, and we'd been writing to each other for two weeks. Every day letters. Sometimes even *more* than every day letters. And now, we couldn't even go a week without seeing each other. We were plotting on the phone right then on how to see each other as soon as possible.

"I have my daughter tonight," Paul said.

"And I've got pottery class Monday and Wednesday nights. What about Tuesday? Do you have Aniela on Tuesday nights?"

"No, I work Tuesday. But maybe I could come over after work?"

"Sure! That'd be great. We could have dinner and watch a movie. Or maybe sit in the hot tub?"

"Yeah. I'd like to sit in the hot tub with you." I could hear the smile in his voice. I grinned to myself.

We decided on "Harold and Maude." I'd never seen it and it was a favorite of Paul's; he wanted to share it with me. We finalized our plans for Tuesday night and hung up. My face was in perpetual grin and I skimmed across the floors with lightness. I loved that excitement and floaty feeling you get when everything seems possible.

I shut off lights as I walked through the house to my bedroom in the back. I checked on both Joey and Aubrey, who were sleeping soundly. I sighed with deliciousness. My babies were so awesome.

As I readied for bed I counted up the suitors I'd actually brought home. Rodney. But he was our neighbor, so probably him coming and going wasn't too confusing for Aubrey. And then there was the guy that broke up with me by mail, and he only lasted two months. When that ended so quickly, I decided I wouldn't have another man stay over until I was really secure in the relationship and I knew he'd be around for a long time. I didn't want Aubrey wondering who "this" or "that" person was. She loved her daddy, and I thought that when Rodney was coming over all the time – putting her to bed, feeding her, playing with her – she might've been subbing Rodney for Rob in her lonely toddler mind.

So.

Paul was coming over for dinner and a movie on Tuesday night. That was fine. Aubrey would meet him as my friend and she'd go to bed at some point and when she woke up he would be gone and it wouldn't interrupt her life.

I nodded to myself and crawled into bed. Decision made.

 Monday, February 25, 2002

> Valerie,
>
> I went to sleep thinking about you, I woke up thinking about you, I dropped my daughter off at school and met a friend for breakfast and I talked about you ... I think I might be in trouble.
>
> I'm looking forward to seeing you tomorrow night. Until then I guess I'll just have to get by with thinking about you.
>
> Paul

Monday was a typical noisy mommy day. Aubrey ladeled sugar onto the kitchen counter and pulled utensils from the drawers. Joey jumped up and down in his exer-saucer and complained about a fever that I'd already dosed up with baby Tylenol. He was really too big for it, but where else do you put a baby when they've got a fever and you're trying to clean house? A Flintstones video played in the background and I listened to a Latin Fiesta CD, which was thankfully louder than the TV. As I wandered through the carnage, I munched graham crackers and sipped at flat Diet Coke.

Yet, all I could do was smile. Nothing could dispel my lovely mood. I wiped up spills, played with my children, made lunches and danced around in my socks. *He's the One. The One* after Rob. I didn't think I'd find another *One*, but our personalities were so similar. When it came to displaying our emotions, we were the same. Our bodies spoke the same language, even though our stories were different. He'd been out of his relationship for six years, me only one and a half. His ended badly, mine ended tragically – well, the crashing into a sign post was tragic. But our emotional needs and wants were twins, sharing the same heart. We were the same.

Paul was mature. He really had it all together. On the outside as well as the inside. He had a job with a great income, owned a house *and* rental properties, and he knew what he wanted. I really craved that stability. I relaxed around Paul. I felt safe around Paul.

I remembered his lips on mine in that awkward first kiss and I wanted to know Paul even more. I wanted his stories. His dreams. His whispers.

After pottery class Monday night, I checked my email first thing to see if he'd sent me anything. I was totally addicted to him already.

Monday, February 25, 2002
Valerie,

I had plans tonight, but they fell through so I will be home and would love to hear your voice. It's 9:15pm and I just finished with my last customer. (I sure hope I'm not here this late tomorrow!)

I had a thought today. I have to be at work by 8:30am on Wednesday and I'm worried that I may get out of here a little later than I'm hoping to. How would you feel about me possibly spending the night tomorrow? It feels like it's a little bit early in the relationship for over night visits but I'd hate to come up and stay for only an hour or so. Think about it.

I'll talk to you when you get home.
Paul

SHIT.

I just made this decision. I wasn't going to let anyone spend the night!

My hand worried over the computer mouse, shaking the cursor over his words.

Damn.

What do I do now?

I looked over at the family room couch. And it's length. Paul's feet would hang over the edge of the arm. The family room was at the opposite end of the house, so if Aubrey saw him in the morning, it wouldn't be him coming out of my bedroom. And maybe he'd be gone before she got up? I shook my head. No way. She was an early riser. 5:30 a.m. usually.

Well.

I *really* wanted to see him.

I held my breath, the decision thwacking back and forth in my brain like a tennis ball at Wimbledon.

I imagined Aubrey and what her reaction would be. Rodney had spent the night before. Many times. And she didn't seem to bat an eyelash. He was my friend and we were just having a sleepover. She'd done that plenty of times with her cousins. And she was a big girl. And so happy all the time. I didn't think it'd scar her. If I did it all the time with different men, that would be different. But it'd just been Rodney, the Two-Monther, and now Paul. And he'd be on the couch, so it'd be even more clear to Aubrey that Paul was just a sleepover friend. No big deal.

I called Paul.

CHAPTER 21

The next morning was beautiful. The late February air was crisp and sunny. I wanted to shout "Hooray!" to the sun. I hoped that Paul wasn't stuck in his office so much that he couldn't appreciate it. That would suck for him.

I dropped the kids at daycare and ran errands most of the day with no coat on and my window rolled down. *India Arie* played on the CD player and I sang loud with my whole lungs. I couldn't stop thinking about seeing Paul that night.

Life was amazing and grand.

When he arrived, the house had been polished up. I was quite proud of my straightening abilities when I had reason to show them off. First impressions were important and I wanted the house to look cool. So that I'd look cool. Okay, that was dumb, but unfortunately, it was true that I thought that way sometimes.

He knocked, and I opened the front door. I smiled and hoped my shirt didn't look stupid with the pants I had on, and that my hair looked okay. He hugged me when he came in and I gave him a tour of the house. He liked it. And then it was time to introduce him to Susan and the children. I was nervous. I wanted Susan to like Paul. I wanted Paul to like my babies.

Of course there was no reason to worry. Susan and Paul smiled, shook hands and talked easily. Aubrey was big-eyed and innocent and on her best behavior. I didn't know why though – I didn't ask her to – but I was thankful all the same. Joey was an itty bitty wonder and so happy and wiggly in his high chair.

Paul excused himself to the bathroom while I finished up feeding the children. Susan and I had started it before Paul arrived – Aubrey at the bar with her food cut up super small and Joey in his chair with his baby food.

After the kids were wiped up and their dishes rinsed out, I let them down to play with their toys for a little bit before bed. I was standing in the kitchen when first Paul's voice, then his body, came out from down the hallway. He was smiling and his face was rosy pink. He gestured with his hands above his head in mock melodrama.

"Do you have a plunger?!" He laughed. "The one thing you should never say the first time you visit a woman's house."

I laughed, too.

"It's in the other bathroom." I went back to my tasks in the kitchen before laughing harder. I didn't want to make him even more horrified than I knew he must be. *Damn*. I would die if our roles were reversed. But he pulled it off with humor and charm. Nice. I nodded to myself – his earned points tallied in my head – and finished wiping out the sink.

We had dinner and I excused myself to put the children to bed. Aubrey was a little love and settled in happily and I gave Joey a bottle in his crib. I gave them both hugs and kisses and I tickled Aubrey's face like she liked when she was all tucked into bed.

Miraculously, there were no further peeps from them and they fell asleep quickly. Susan disappeared into her bedroom for studying and Paul and I snuggled on the couch to watch *Harold and Maude*. After the movie, I checked the hot tub water's temperature (I had just added new water that morning), and despite the late hour, we contemplated getting in.

"I was really hoping to get a look at you in your swimsuit," Paul said. He grinned like a fourteen-year-old. Sharky and sweet at the same time. I laughed and felt equally self-conscious and sexy.

"Okay. Are you sure it's not too late for you?" I asked.

"I'm fine."

IN THE HOT TUB WE PRETENDED TO CONVERSE, BUT REALLY WE JUST wanted an excuse to touch each other. He draped his arms on the rim of the tub. I moved around the different seats, pretending I was trying to get comfortable. We ended up holding hands under water and sitting side by side on one of the benches. We talked in the darkness for a little while, but soon enough, Paul was sitting cross-legged at the bottom of the tub and I was sitting on his lap with my legs wrapped around his waist.

I hugged him and stayed there, nestled in his arms and felt the safety and aura of being cherished. It was a heady feeling.

"You look amazing in your suit, by the way."

"Thank you." I would've said more but he kissed me and it was *not* awkward and I kissed him back. Hard.

We rocked in each other's arms and wriggled and squirmed and slid hands over skin and kissed and kissed and kissed. My face tingled and every muscle in my body was tight with anticipation and fear and desire.

"I like that you bite your bottom lip when you get excited," he whispered.

I bit my lip without thinking. And then we laughed. It released the tension and I felt normal again. I lay against his chest.

"I feel safe in your arms," I said.

"Well, I hope so," he chuckled. He kissed me again. Slow this time. And tender. With both hope and promises behind it. "I really want to make love to you, Valerie."

My breath caught. I wanted it, too. But this was only our second date. What would he think of me if I did? What would *I* think of me if I did? The last guy I said 'no' to didn't ever see me again. I didn't want Paul to go away. I looked into his sensitive eyes. Again a wash of relief and safety cleansed my heart. I knew that the man sitting with me in that hot tub would never leave a woman after only ten days of knowing her because she wouldn't have sex with him.

I kissed him. And hugged him. And quickly whispered in his ear, "I'm afraid," and then kissed him again before he could answer back – a strange rendition of me confessing my love for Rob.

"Why?" He was concerned and held me gently.

I tried to laugh it off.

"I don't know, really." I smiled to soften any disappointment. "I'm just not sure. It's so early, you know? I'm just scared." *Scared of going so fast even though I love the excitement and adrenaline of it. Scared of how strongly I feel about you. Scared of falling in love again. And being hurt again.*

"It's okay," Paul said. He pulled me into his arms. All safety and strong and manly. "It's okay. We don't have to." He stroked my hair and hugged me tight.

Inside we huddled in our wet towels and looked down at the couch.

"I'll get some blankets for you."

He looked at me and then at the couch.

"It's actually longer than my bed," I laughed. "There's no way you'd fit in my bed. It's a double-sized and it has a footboard. At least with this you could hang your feet over." I gestured to the couch.

"I've had these long legs all my life. I'm used to making myself fit in spaces that aren't big enough for me." He smiled. "I can lay diagonally." He pulled me to him and kissed my forehead. "I want to sleep next to you."

I was so over sleeping alone. I hated the empty bed. I wanted a warm, sleeping body next to mine at night. I wanted to sleep with my head on his shoulder and my arm slung over his chest. I wanted to feel him breathing next to me.

I thought of Aubrey.

Would having Paul spend the night be weird or scary for her? Would it be confusing for her? Would she be scarred by having "Mommy's Man Friends" around? She missed Rob. That I knew. And Rodney wasn't around a lot anymore. I knew she missed him, too. My other dates that had come over casually for a movie or something had been minimal, but still. Was it confusing her? Up until a couple of weeks ago, she was still waiting for Rob to come back from heaven!

I sighed and closed my eyes and leaned back into Paul. I didn't want to think about it anymore. I worried so much about Aubrey. But maybe I worried too much. Aubrey would take from it what I put out there. If I treated Paul spending the night as a friendly sleepover and nothing more – even if it felt more to me – then that was how Aubrey would perceive it. Casual. Normal. No big deal. She wouldn't attach any importance to it until I wanted her to.

At least I hoped so. Because it dawned on me that I wasn't the only one dating other men; Aubrey was too. Aubrey was part of me. Part of my family. Part of the package. If I was hurt in a relationship, chances were Aubrey would be, too. So I needed to be vigilant. And protective.

But sometimes I felt tired. Sometimes I wanted to be the protected, instead of the protector. Sometimes I just wanted arms around me and to not sleep in an empty bed.

I caved.

Right there in the family room.

"Okay," I said. My voice was subdued. I didn't feel bullied into it. It was something I wanted. It was just that all of a sudden my micro-relationship with Paul got very important somehow.

And important in what way, I wasn't sure. But something was different. Not wrong. Just – something.

I wondered if I would be able to sleep with him there. I checked on the kids before getting into bed with Paul. They were both lovely cherubs and the image of them sleeping stayed with me even as Paul wrapped his arms around me and spooned me close to him.

In the morning, we woke at the same time and Paul wrapped me up in his arms again. He breathed in my hair.

"The only thing better than falling asleep with you is waking up next to you."

Awwww.

My heart melted on the spot and I smiled a sleepy, snuggly smile.

His hand stroked my arm and my back and my hip … and then cupped my breast.

Whoa.

Did I want this? Yes, my body shouted at me. Did I feel safe with this? Yes, my body shouted at me. Will this hurt anybody? No, my body shouted at me. *Okay, okay! I just needed to check in. Sheesh, already.* And so I turned towards Paul and reciprocated his attentions.

"Are you sure? You're not scared anymore?"

"I'm not scared anymore." I felt a little shy though. But emboldened by his desire all the same. We stroked each other and re-positioned and melted into one. Again and again.

And then.

Aubrey opened the door to my room.

We froze under the covers.

I smiled over at her.

"Good morning, Sweetie. Go out into the family room and I'll be right there, Punkin."

No expression. Her hand dropped off the doorknob and she turned like a ghost and walked away.

Paul and I looked at each other.

"Shit," I said. Then I smiled at Paul, a little apologetically. "Good morning," I offered.

He smiled, pulled out and we got up. He hopped into the shower and I pulled on a robe and went to the family room. None of the lights were on along the way. I started to call out to Aubrey but then I saw her.

SHE WAS SITTING
    in the dark
    in the very center
    of the couch.
    Her back was to me.

MY HEART DROPPED TO MY DIAPHRAGM. SOMETHING WAS WRONG. I sat down next to her, kissed the top of her head and touched her arm to see if she was cold.

"Good morning, my baby girl," I said with sweetness and warmth in my voice.

Her response cut daggers in me.

"I miss Daddy."

CHAPTER 22

I held her tightly to me and rocked her. I didn't dare speak yet, for fear I would cry and make her feel more confused and sad than she already appeared to be.

"Oh, baby," I murmured. I snuggled her into my lap. She wrapped her arms around my waist and pressed her ear against my heart.

"I miss him, too." I looked out the sliding glass door to the early morning light. My heartbeat was steady. It was safe. Always there. No change. Could she hear it? I hoped it brought her peace. I held her until she wanted down.

When Paul was out of the shower I handed him a cup of coffee.

"There's no such thing as too much sugar in coffee," he said when I told him I might've put too much in.

Paul made fried eggs with seasoning salt for us and we ate all fancy in the dining room. I even pulled in Joey's highchair so he could join us and then worried the whole time about messes on the rug under the table. He'd been coughing for days and though he was hungry, he only moved the food around on his tray half-heartedly.

After the kids were done, I released them to the family room and the Disney channel. Paul and I puttered with the dishes and he put his shoes on. I averted my face so he didn't see my expression. He was wearing white sneakers with brown corduroy pants and I didn't know whether to laugh or grimace. He looked like he was headed to the golf course.

He noticed anyway.

"I had on my Dockers yesterday. My sneakers look good with the Dockers," he insisted, and asked if there was a Fred Meyer nearby where he could get some dress shoes before he went to work.

"Yes." The muscles in my face contorted in an effort not to laugh outright. I gave him directions.

"Do you want another cup of coffee?" I asked.

"Sure." He came up behind me with his mug and slid his hand across my shoulders and down my arm. I smiled and turned away from the coffee pot towards him.

"I love having coffee with you in the morning," I said, "and I miss sleeping next to someone. It was nice. I'm glad you stayed." I pulled out of the embrace, our hands still intertwined, and looked into his eyes. He seemed shy and looked down at our hands. He smiled with sweetness and pulled me back in. My insides felt full to bursting. My lips stretched and my eyes crinkled in a permanent smile.

After he left, I bounced around with the kids and they reveled in my happiness. Aubrey and I giggled together and poor Joey coughed, but he smiled all the same.

I wondered if Rob would have approved of Paul. I'd never asked him. I shook my head. Who's to say that Rob could even approve or disapprove anything from where he was – whether he said so or not in my journal? I sighed. And did it really matter? I was here. I needed to make decisions and choices for myself and for my children. No one else. Dead or living.

I didn't feel guilty that day for having romantic and sexual interest in someone who wasn't Rob. Other days I did, but that day, no. It felt real and safe and the right thing to do. For me, and for Aubrey and Joey. They needed a male figure – a dad – in their lives. An email from Paul later that morning further solidified my euphoria and sense that Paul was the real deal.

> Wednesday, February 27, 2002
> Valerie,
> It's astonishing the way I feel like I know you so well after such a short time.
> Thank you for making me feel alive again. Thank you for making me feel so joyous that I can't stop smiling. Thank you for coming into my life and just being who you are. Thank you. Thank you. Thank you.
> With great passion and joy,
> Paul

I RELUCTANTLY LEFT THE COMPUTER – I WANTED TO CRAFT A RESPONSE but needed to get Joey ready for a doctor's appointment. His cough just wasn't going away. Probably I'd get there and they'd say it was a cold and to let it ride. I'd feel stupid for being worried over a wee cold and I'd probably wish that I'd waited it out a couple more days. But. Better to be safe than sorry, and I needed to get back to school or I'd fail my math class. I couldn't go if Joey was sick, so I felt better just checking in with the pediatrician.

It turned out to be an excellent notion.

Joey had Respiratory Syncytial Virus. RSV. The RSV had developed into bronchiolitis, too. Oh. And an ear infection. Lovely. Joey needed to have four breathing treatments a day with a nebulizer. Hopefully for only a week.

I rented the nebulizer and got all the meds, with the two little ones in tow. I straggled into the family room from the garage – diaper bag and Joey, my purse and the bag of medicine all balanced in my arms. I went back for a second trip to get the nebulizer. I didn't want to drop the box and break the unit.

The first treatment went something like this: Plug in the unit, pour in the medicine, sit ten-month-old Joey on my lap, try to put the oxygen mask-looking thing on his nose and mouth with the elastic band around his head, struggle with him, get it firmly on, hold his hands away from his face, turn on the unit (it was LOUD), make smiley faces and bounce my knee to distract my baby and try to turn it into a game.

His eyes were wide and startled and he hated the mask. He fussed and then started coughing. Deep, wet, gagging coughs. He arched his back and tried to scream through his coughing. I pulled off the mask and turned off the unit. I didn't want to waste the medicine.

I soothed Joey and wiped his face and distracted him with toys and he fussed. He was probably tired, and he just didn't feel good. My soul ached for him. He was so sick. I turned on *The Wiggles* – his favorite show – and set him on my lap again. I turned on the nebulizer and held the mask in front of his face but didn't touch his skin. When he moved his face, I moved the mask. I followed him wherever he turned. I sang *Wiggles* songs and tried to distract him until the treatment was over. It took about fifteen minutes.

When I turned it off, the silence slammed into my eardrums. For such a disagreeable medical treatment, especially for little babies who didn't understand what was going on, you'd think they could make a quieter machine.

I put Joey down and he relaxed while I got the area cleaned up. Lunchtime was next and then naps. For all. Today would most assuredly be a nap day for me, too. With only one hour of sleep last night, and the sickening stress at the doctor's office, I was dragging. I ached for Paul and so wanted his arms around me in a strong solid hug.

Only after I climbed into bed for my own nap, did I realize that I had wished for *Paul's* arms – and not Rob's. Remembering my time with Paul last night, I recalled holding his face in my hands. I loved so many things about him already, like how he put my unspoken thoughts to words. Thoughts I hadn't shared yet, but he somehow knew all the same.

I loved that he had suggested "sleepovers" throughout the week. It was reminiscent of *Big* with Tom Hanks.

Mostly I loved that he'd already found a place in my life and in my heart.

"Please don't go away," I whispered to my pillow. And then I slept until Aubrey woke up from her nap.

THE NEXT MORNING I ACKNOWLEDGED, UNWILLINGLY, THAT I couldn't take Joey to daycare. With him sick, I couldn't risk him getting the other kids sick, and that meant no school for me again. Maybe I'd do some yard work. I still needed to go grocery shopping, too. Blah. I hated grocery shopping. Especially with the two little ones along.

I posted a quick email to Paul, letting him know that my plans had changed and that I was home that day in case he wanted to call me. I hit send and then turned to Aubrey.

LATER THAT NIGHT I WROTE PAUL AGAIN. JUST BRIEFLY SO HE DIDN'T think I was stalking him. Though at this point, early as it was in our dating, based on his email responses, I felt fairly confident that he didn't mind me slathering all my attention on him. I think he liked it and I felt so blessed and lucky. I knew I could be a little intense and that some people were really scared off by that. It was so wonderful that Paul wasn't, and I felt a sob of gratitude pushing up my throat. I swallowed it back and typed.

CHAPTER 23

I didn't sleep well during the night and I struggled with fuzziness the next morning. After breakfast I got the kiddos interested in their toys, and – full disclosure – the TV, and I went into the living room with my journal. I wanted to collect some thoughts that had been rambling for a few days.

Rob.

How could I *not* think of him? He was ever present. Even when I was with Paul. I didn't think it would always be that way. I didn't think I'd be married to Paul years later and have Rob still be in the room while I kissed Paul. But for right now... he was.

I checked in with myself. My eyes closed, deep breath, the pen poised over the page. Was it okay that Rob was still here? Did I *want* him to go away? I didn't want to ever forget Rob. But was it rational that if I wasn't thinking of him all the time, that I'd be forgetting him?

And where did Paul really fit in here? Would he blend well with our family? He *said* he didn't mind that Rob was still a part of our lives, but would he be able to make his own place with us? Would he love Aubrey and Joey as his own children? Or would he play favorites with his daughter, Aniela? That seemed so easy to do, and really, I could understand if he did – favor Aniela – but I needed to find a man that would stand by my kids and love them and hold them forever close to his heart. I didn't want them to ever feel unloved because their father died.

I didn't even know what to write in my journal. My pen swirled in my fingers and I forced the tip to the page and watched the ink seep in, a small blob at first, but then spreading, like blood through veins.

I felt restless. I wanted to sink into Paul and not think. I just wanted to be with him. I wanted him to love me and my children.

My breath stopped for a second.

Did I love him?

Maybe. I didn't know yet.

It was too noisy to think by then. The kids were distracting me. I gave up on the journaling and went back to the family room with them.

I TOLD PAUL I LOVED HIM IN BED ONE NIGHT, SOME WEEKS LATER. I knew he heard me because he sighed and squeezed me to him. I asked him anyway.

"Did you hear me?"

"Yes."

Oh.

"I don't know what to say. I'm still processing this amazing time I'm spending with you. I love spending time with you. I'm just not ready to say it back yet," he said.

"That's okay. It's my gift to you. That's all."

"Thank you," he murmured and snuggled, and we slept.

A WEEK LATER I MET HIS MOTHER, ANNA, FOR THE FIRST TIME. IT IS pronounced Ah-na, not Ann-a. She had eighteen acres of trees in Roseburg, Oregon. She bought eighteen acres of trees so that none of them could ever be chopped down. It turned out I'd found another kindred soul.

I hadn't meant to meet her that day, but our schedules all opened at the same time for once, and Paul asked me to meet them at the mall in Springfield for lunch. I had just colored my hair that morning and, to my dismay, it turned out carrot orange.

She didn't even bat an eyelash when she saw it.

I had forgotten a bottle for Joey in my haste to be on time, so Paul walked through the mall to Target and bought him one. After a long meal, the kids got antsy, so we ended up driving to Paul's place. We stayed a lot longer than we anticipated and decided to sleep over as a result.

Joey's playpen was still there from a previous sleepover, so while Aubrey and Aniela played *Shrek* on the Xbox, and Anna sat on the couch and read a book, and Paul fed Joey a bottle, I rustled around getting things "set."

I put Joey down to sleep in Paul's bedroom, while Paul cooked up something for dinner. When I came out of the bedroom, frazzled from Joey's tears and frustration at not wanting to fall asleep, I could hear the girls and their video game. I looked at Paul in the kitchen. He leaned up against the counter and crossed his arms.

"I'm sorry," I mouthed.

He tilted his head and his brows scrunched together.

"The noise and the chaos." I shrugged my shoulders in apology.

His face smoothed out and he opened his arms to me. I walked into them. I smelled his deodorant and Paul smell through his green plaid shirt. My cheek rested against his chest.

"I love you," he whispered.

My blood jumped and I lifted my face so I could see his eyes. His lovely hazel eyes – made more green by his shirt. He was serious. I laughed. The kids arguing, Joey fussing, scrounging for dinner at the last minute, his *mom* in the next room, my hair and clothes were rumpled from the day – and he said 'I love you' *then*?

"Why did you say that now?"

He shrugged with a goofy smile.
"I just felt it," he said.
And then we kissed.
Until I remembered, with embarrassment, that his mom was in the next room.

PART III

Dancing in the Rain

(Four Years Later)

> Dear Rob,

I wonder what you would think of me now. If you were here, what would we talk about? Before, we talked mostly of our love, about work and about moving into our own place. We talked of love and passion and blow jobs. We talked of silly jokes and military life and I listened to you speak to me in Portuguese – a language I never learned but still think of trying every now and again.

But what would we talk of now? What I've been doing since you left, most likely. How funny. Saying 'you left' sounds like you took a job in Alaska instead of dying five hours after I discovered my pregnancy with Joey. Your last gift. My last child.

Though sometimes I still wish I could have more. Adopt or – anything. But Paul doesn't want anymore and (maybe) it wouldn't be the same anyway. Because it's occurred to me that maybe I want more children so I can be reminded of the life I no longer have with you. It's a way of missing you, of missing something that hadn't happened yet; a dream we had together. Do you remember that you wanted seven children?

I still smile at that. We could've done it – you and me. And all your Portuguese family. That family is mine, too, if I allow it.

I'm not close to your family, Rob. Oh, it's not intentional. It's not a conscious attempt to block them out. It's the same with all friends I've moved away from. We just migrate. Lose touch. Though your mom won't allow that too much. She still calls once a week, or so, and checks in. I'm glad she does.

Joey actually talked to her yesterday. He doesn't like to talk to her on the phone usually. It may just be that he won't be a phone person. Or maybe he blames her for his homesickness when he spent a month in Massachusetts this summer. Who knows? I'm awed at how much I don't know about our children.

There it is again, Rob. "Our" children. They are as much Paul's children as yours, yet I feel compelled to call them 'our' children when I talk to you, and 'our' children when I talk to Paul. It's weird. I guess they really are all "our" children. All three of ours. You fathered them in the biblical sense – biologically. But Paul's been the dad for so many years now.

So maybe I should tell you about this Paul guy: He loves them. He truly does. He hangs with them, holds them when they're sad or hurt, kisses them god-night and plays with them.

He *does* work long hours and wishes to spend more time with them, so he's started going into work a little late – stealing minutes to give back to Aubrey and Joey.

Aubrey's still a daddy's girl – though not as much as with you when she was twenty months old. She likes school, Harry Potter, magic, fairies, music and art. She's still in choir and yesterday I watched her dance with my scarf by the side of the road. There was a parade and music was playing in the streets. She's at once self-conscious, *and* courageously artistically spiritual. She's at home with who she is but can, and will, weep when she feels unjustly used or put upon.

She is me. But looks like you. Paul said one day that "Aubrey always looked like Aubrey. In her baby pictures – she always looked like her." And Paul is right, too. It's true. She still looks like her baby pictures – yet I see glimpses of the young woman that is coming fast. Before I'm ready, I fear.

Joey looks more like my mom's side of the family. So more of me. And he's an Aries sign – just like me. And he's got a fire-y temper that burns off fairly quickly – just like me. But I suspect he has a lot more of you in him. Interesting things that I pause and wonder at. Like, he has imaginary friends – tons of them – but not tin the sweet "isn't that cute?" way. More like the goblins hiding in the closet to steal the baby in that move "The Labyrinth." Though in a sad way – not evil.

He has a 'friend' that, I suspect, correlates to each different facet of his personality. Fun Boy, Punching Boy, Quiet Boy, Skateboarding Boy.

When his temper and frustrations get the better of him (as happens often), he gets rough and aggressive with the people he's around. No matter if they are adults, children or pets. Afterwards he feels bad about it and seeks comfort from me. When I talk to him about it, he says peculiar things about his "friends." His "friend" told him to do it. His *mind* told him to do it – not *him*. And for a couple of months, his "friends" wanted him dead. It was quite alarming actually. I've wondered if he could be depressed like you and your grandfathers were. It does run in the family. I watch and wonder. And wait.

Joey tries to "feed the good wolf," as he put it one day after a friend used that expression. But sometimes he's just not successful. Poor kid. He loves snakes, sharks, Tom and Jerry, and bugs. But not bees.

And now I'm wondering about me. And you. I wonder if you'd like me now. Resonate with who I am and what I stand for *now*. I'm *still* not Catholic – though I did have Joey baptized to carry on the tradition, so to speak. And to soothe your mom.

Me. Who am I now? Well, I dated a little after Joey was born. I journaled a lot. I treated myself monthly to nurturing pedicures and massages. I bought a house and had it fixed up. And I met Paul. (I think you know him from other lives, Rob.)

I went to massage school and I'm a licensed massage therapist now. I'm serious about my writing and I've got a bit of art on the walls and shelves around my house. After you died, I did a lot of my healing in art. I worked with clay and dabbled in painting and *always* wrote. I meditated and journaled and channeled and cried and healed. I tried to parent as best I knew how, with the strength I had. And Paul helped.

We share things, Paul and I. He'd parent when I was sick or at school; I'd parent when he'd had a bad day at work. Paul encourages me to continue expressing myself creatively and never nags at me to do the housework.

Do you remember the time you said, "What do you *do* all day?" You were looking at the toys on the floor, the unmade bed and the dishwasher half-loaded. Paul never does that.

I remember other things, too. I remember your giggle when you were excited. It wasn't your regular laugh you shared with everyone else, it was the one you only used with me, when you were being tickled. It was the giggle you giggled when I showed you the pregnancy test for Joey. You jumped up and down in the bathroom, penis flopping. Giggling.

I hugged you – "We're having a baby."

But now? If I was pregnant right now with your baby I'd still hug you and say "We're having a baby." But it would be different. I'd do it based on who I am now.

Cloth diapers, breastfeeding for at *least* a year, organic baby food, no plastic toys – only wood and natural materials like organic wool, silk and organic cotton. Natural dyes, Waldorf-y toys. Homeschool. *Unschool.*

I'm homeschooling Joey – did I tell you? I think you'd approve.

Oh, and I have prayer flags on my front porch and goddess flags in my living room. I rarely watch TV and I mow the lawn with a push reel mower – no gasoline. I recycle. I compost. I use no harsh cleaners (no more bleach for your warts). I even bike when I can, instead of drive, and hang the clothes outside to dry. Organic everything if I have the choice, homeopathic or naturopathic medicine only. Alternative diets and yoga.

Yeah. My life has changed a bit since I've known you.

But I still miss you. And I still wish we were together. I love you.

Love, Valerie

CHAPTER 24

Aubrey's hair was just grazing the bottom of her ears and the back of her neck – a new haircut for a new seven-year-old. She was silently eating her peanut butter and jelly sandwich, with a frothy glass of chocolate milk beside her. She had on a lime green tee-shirt and grinned with expressive eyebrows.

Four-year-old Joey was building train tracks in his room upstairs. I could see his doorway from the kitchen of our split-level.

And Aniela, now fourteen, sat at the computer, a bowl of rice and a Coke can beside her – despite the "no drinks by the keyboard" rule.

Paul was at work and our not-so-new-anymore mixed-breed puppy, Montana, was wandering around the family room. I eyed her, watching to see if she'd pee on the carpet again. She was super smart, just not in the potty-training department.

I'd been feeling anxious again. I suspected my health was a contributing factor.

Something was off. Maybe I had food allergies. I felt weak and tired a lot. Mostly I wanted to read and sleep. Or watch movies.

Sometimes I felt single, even though I had a loving partner sleeping next to me every night. I felt disconnected. Not just from

Paul, but everyone. I didn't seem to get close to people. Girlfriends were held at length; I kept myself busy with volunteer work so I didn't notice that I had no close friends. I wasn't even close to myself in those days.

Maybe it was just winter.
I hibernated in the winter.
Like a bear with crust in its eyes
And grumbly from lack of sleep.

There was a distance between Paul and I. I didn't know who manufactured it, myself or him. Was it his computer gaming? He had assured me when we first started dating that he didn't play very much, *like Rob did*, but that didn't turn out to be so accurate. Was it that I'd denied my feelings for Rob's death and my loss, and therefore denied my feelings for Paul?

I'd felt this distance for some time, like everything was vague and frosty. Like on auto-pilot, just going through the motions. And I was afraid of what that meant.

It was the highest form of denial – pretending the gap between us didn't exist. Ignoring it. Hoping maybe it'd go away.

I had a painting class that night. *That* was something. A window in the box I found myself in in those days – self-imposed, I was sure. And I'd started a new book. *The Memory Keeper's Daughter* by Kim Edwards.

While the children and puppy were all engaged, and each one of them were in my peripheral vision, hope and despair battled. For the moment, that lovely moment in the kitchen with my daughter – watching her eat a peanut butter sandwich – hope beat out mightier and I found an inkling of inner strength. *I would find Me in the things I liked to do. I would open up with the people around me more. Including Paul. And I would think about Rob when I wanted to and not feel guilty about it.*

There. I just committed to myself, and I felt my shoulders lower away from my ears. My spirits rose ... and then fell just as quick. Because not feeling guilty about thinking about Rob was hard to do.

Paul felt bad when I thought of Rob, despite Paul's assertion at the beginning of our relationship that he knew I "had a past," and that he wasn't the first guy to date me. Still, I didn't want him thinking I thought of Rob all the time.

On one occasion, I had been washing dishes, looking out the window to the back yard. The little kids were at the dining room table eating and coloring; Aniela was with her mom that week. Paul was playing music. He found a song he liked and played it for me.

"Listen to this," he said. "It's by Marc Cohn."

It was a song called "True Companion."

"It's got a funny story behind it," he said. "He'd just finished writing it and wanted to try it out on his girlfriend. Have her listen to it. So he did and during the song, while he was singing it to her, she started crying and said, 'Yes! Yes, I'll marry you!'" Paul shook his head and chuckled. "He was so surprised. That wasn't what he intended at all. He wasn't proposing."

I looked down at the sink and blinked rapidly. The sudsy water clung to my wrists and I rinsed off the bowl I was washing under the tap. I set it in the drying rack. I looked back out the window and opened my eyes wide to dry them out, praying that tears wouldn't fall.

He wasn't proposing.

Just like Paul.

He wasn't proposing either.

Paul and I still weren't married. We'd been together for four years and he wouldn't marry me. He said he didn't need a piece of paper from the government saying that he was committed to our relationship. He already was.

And I would lose some of my government issued income if we got married.

But not getting married because I would lose money made me feel like a whore. Somehow. I knew it didn't make a lot of sense, but … I still felt un-loved and "not good enough" because we weren't married.

The tears fell anyway. Despite my attempts otherwise.

Wasn't I already Paul's "true companion?" Why did I need the marriage certificate?

Paul swayed up behind me, dancing to the music. He wrapped himself around me from behind. I must have stiffened, because he pulled back and turned me around. His face fell.

"What's wrong?" His shoulders fell, too. "You're thinking of Rob, aren't you?"

Confusion. Disbelief. Irritation.

"No!" I wiped the tears from my face in swipes. "I was …" But I couldn't say what I had thought. We'd already talked about it so often, and I didn't want to nag.

And another time. More proof that Paul was sad when I thought of Rob.

It was Paul's birthday and we'd gone out to the movies. His choice. It wasn't a movie I wanted to see, but it was his birthday. The movie he chose was the incredibly depressing *Cold Mountain*.

After the movie, in the car, I was sobbing.

"What was the *point* of that? How could you think that was a remotely romantic movie?"

"His love for her was the only thing that got him through the war. It was the only thing that kept him alive and got him home." Paul was impassioned and alive and flushed with enthusiasm.

"But he died! *Right* when he got home. *Right* when she saw him again. It was terrible! There was no point to it."

"Of course there was a point to it," he explained. His voice was calm now and soothing. "Maybe there wasn't a point that you saw. Or a point the woman saw. But there was a point for the man. She was his reason for living. There was definitely a point for him."

I sniffled and wiped my face. I found a tissue box in the bottom of the car between the seats and blew my nose.

"You know," I nodded, "I think you might be right. There's

always a point. There's always a reason for something, even if I don't see it."

I looked out over the dash at the other parked cars. Lined up. Waiting to be driven home.

"I think that Rob and I met for a reason. Even if it was for such a short time." I nodded again and looked at Paul. I tried for a smile. It was such a relief to talk to someone like Paul. He always put things in perspective for me. His way of looking at the world helped me stay grounded – something I was eternally grateful for. For while I liked jumping off figurative buildings in a single bound, it was exhausting sometimes and I often lost sight of what I was leaping after. Paul helped with that.

"Yep," he said and looked down at his lap.

I started the van and drove us home.

The babysitter left. I checked on the sleeping kids, and Paul and I went to bed. He turned away from me.

That didn't feel like snuggle-in-bed-after-a-nice-dinner-and-sad-movie-and-connecting-in-the-van-afterwards moment. What was wrong?

I put my hand on his shoulder.

"Are you okay?"

Pause, and then a muffled, 'Yes.'

I ran my hand down his back toward his hips in a suggestive manner. He reached over and captured my fingers on their way back up.

"I'm not really in the mood, Val."

Surprised.

"Oh. Okay." I spooned up next to him and I listened to him breathe. But it didn't sound like the breathing I was used to. "Are you sure you're okay?"

He rolled over on his back. He was crying.

"It's just that. It's my birthday. And when we were talking about the movie and I was sharing with you how much the movie meant to me, you turned it into something about Rob. You were thinking about Rob and I was thinking about you."

"Oh, baby. I wasn't crying about Rob. I wasn't even thinking about Rob during the movie. The only time I thought of him was at the end there when you said that thing about there being a point, and I was reminded of my belief that everything has a reason. And then I thought of Rob being in my life for a reason. I wouldn't have thought of him otherwise."

Paul was silent.

"I promise," I said.

He snorted, and I could feel him shake his head.

"It's my birthday," he said again.

I sighed and rolled onto my back. I looked at the ceiling. I felt frustrated. And unable to even watch a movie where someone dies without my partner thinking I was remembering Rob. Like it was a bad thing.

I sought out shapes in the ceiling's orange peel surface.

Maybe it was.

CHAPTER 25

One morning the children were still sleeping and Paul was in the shower. I hurried to get a cup of coffee so I could sit in the quiet room and continue my waking up ritual before the little ones were up. Aniela was at her mom's that week. The chair I sat in gobbled me up and I sank into my depression.

Last night had been hideous. Paul and I talked about my unhappiness. Despite my love for Paul, something was not quite right. Maybe with me. When I looked around me I saw failure, blandness and oatmeal. But yet ... there was still magic. Could that oatmeal be coming from within me? Or was it in our house – growing in the walls, exhaling from the carpets? Paul was sad and I'm sure felt backed up against a wall, because he started sounding defensive during our conversation. Talk of breaking up was even mentioned.

I hated this place I was in. I nagged and complained and criticized and sucked out all the energy from Paul's field. Like an energy vampire greedily licking my fingers wanting more, never satisfied. And then I'd have the sick realization, the next day, of how I'd acted towards my family.

I started our conversation last night thinking I was doing a good thing – reaching out, showing Paul my vulnerability by asking for help to change and not be so negative.?

But when Paul answered, it was with exhausted patience. Like I was asking yet another thing from him. I felt small and hard and not worth it.

When did I become so negative and cynical? When did I lose my hopefulness? I didn't think it was after Rob's death. My grief over his death was over. But maybe my grief over the death of our *dreams* still lingered. The dreams of growing old together. The dream of continuing to see how much love he had for Aubrey, of feeling his love for me explode in the room when he walked in.

Why didn't I feel that with Paul? Did he not love me as much as Rob did? Or was that not true at all, and that those feelings of lack all stemmed from me? Did *I* no longer have the ability to feel love of that magnitude?

When I met Paul I felt strong love. I had it then; I had the hopefulness of new love, the shine in my eyes, the excitement, the exuberance. So it wasn't that I couldn't feel it, it just left somehow.

Of course, maybe this wasn't about love or grief at all. Maybe it was about happiness. Because I could remember being married to Rob and feeling sick sometimes in my cells, about 'what ifs' always lurking in the back of my mind.

What if I were hurt/raped/mugged? What if Aubrey was kidnapped? What if Rob died? What if I died? What if cheetahs crashed through our bedroom window and tore us up while we slept?

Always lurking in the back of my mind during the most perfect of days was this fear. It tainted everything so that I felt I could never be truly happy. I kept waiting for the "other shoe to drop." When Rob died I felt like, "Well, that was the shoe." I certainly wasn't happy after that, but somehow relieved that nothing bad could ever happen again – because the shoe had finally dropped.

The fear wasn't so strong anymore and sometimes it seemed gone. A bit of sadness bloomed though, like a decoration. I wore that corsage for a while, and then I met Paul. Off came the corsage.

Then the sadness was more nostalgia, and I willingly accepted the excitement of love and the promises of happiness and nurturing – the sadness whispered rather than called out.

So where did the cynicism leak in? What tainted my happiness now?

Paul emerged from the upstairs all showered and dressed for work. He sat on the couch and put on his shoes. He was in work mode; I could see it. I stayed quiet and watched him, sipping my coffee.

He went to the kitchen and I followed him.

"Do you want the leftovers from last night for your lunch today?" I asked.

"Yes. Sure." He poured himself a cup of coffee in a travel mug and I helped him find the lid. I handed him his lunch.

We walked to the front door. He handed me everything while he put on his jacket and took his keys off the hook by the door. I passed his things back to him and kissed him good-bye. I went to look out the big window and waved to him as he backed out of the driveway.

He power-smiled through the window and I blew him a kiss.

MONTHS AND MONTHS PASSED IN A HAZE OF DEPRESSION, HOPE, LOVE, despair, tears and laughter. I even went to a doctor, feeling that *something* just wasn't right. Turns out, I was correct. I was relieved to discover I *did* have health problems. Funny to say that, but there it was. I was *glad* I had Hashimoto's Disease. That meant I took a pill every day and my depression – a by-product of hypothyroidism – mostly went away. I never knew depression was a side effect of a whacked endocrine system. Huh. Now maybe I could feel passion and zest again. Now maybe I could return to the woman I was when I met Paul, and fell in love.

The kids and I were at Anna's place one weekend, just for fun, and I was ruminating on how so much had happened in the four years our families had been together.

So much beauty and so much pain.

Paul did end up proposing. It was on a Christmas Day. After we were done opening presents, he said he had one more for me. He knelt down and opened the ring box, just like in the movies. I laughed and cried and said 'Yes.' But a tiny sliver of rot inside me suggested that he really didn't want to. He was just doing it to appease me. I had *talked him into it*.

I looked out at Anna's trees. If you were quiet enough you might hear the sound of elven children laughing with sparkling eyes. Or hear the solemn wisdom of the nobles while you breathed in the hush that settled around the trees. Forests and trees never ceased to cause great rushes of wonderment and awe for me. The children were inside with Anna, and I was sitting outside in the sun with my journal, looking at trees and getting to know myself again.

There was such happiness and beauty in my life since I'd started my medication, that my inadequate human parameters almost couldn't bear it. Tears threatened to spill over, and sometimes did.

Wasn't it amazing that were so many facets of human emotion, yet when those emotions rose to their fullest peak there was only one option if you didn't want to choke on them. To cry. It seemed a strange way to share great happiness or to describe the awe at nature's beauty. What a funny way to honor beauty – to cry.

I supposed I shouldn't feel ashamed at the literal out-pouring of emotion and passion in the form of tears. It was merely another way of expressing that passion felt.

When there were no words, at least there were tears.

The entrance to the forest beckoned and I got up from the grassy field and wandered closer, my journal tucked under my arm.

My deep love for Paul was intoxicating and somehow, out

SMELL THE BLUE SKY

there, I felt it grow stronger. As if I were more myself on Anna's property amongst the trees, and so therefore felt that love grow roots and mingle with the forest. I wandered and explored, smelled and heard the sweet grass crunch beneath my feet. My jeans whispered where I walked.

I wanted to sit with Paul right then and watch the trees grow and see the grass dance. To feel him beside me, so strong and sure. Caring and loving, supportive. To breathe in the breeze as it tickled our hair and danced in our eyelashes. But he was at work.

I wanted to hold onto this hope and love and togetherness I felt in that forest. To tether myself to it.

Because other times – a lot more times than I cared to admit – our days were shadowed by something not so rosy. Because even then, four years after I met him and we'd bought a house together, I found myself sad that Rob was not there. And I agonized that maybe my ability to love a man was stunted somehow from the trauma of my loss.

Therapists and counselors told me that perhaps I hadn't yet grieved Rob's death, that I'd kept myself too busy. I supposed that could be true, yet it didn't seem quite accurate. It was true that I was embarrassed by my grief. I was shamed by it and felt guilty even for the shame. For didn't that shame Rob then?

I loved Paul. So, so much. But. How could I love Paul, if I still missed Rob?

The sun beat on my head where I'd sat back down again in the field. I closed my journal and my eyes. I tilted my face to the sun and took deep reassuring breaths. I didn't want to go inside feeling jittery, so I chased the demons away by looking at the trees for a few more minutes. A bird soared above me and swooped, just to feel the wind as it danced beneath him. I smiled.

CHAPTER 26

I finally finished my book. It took so much longer to read a novel as a parent with animals and a disreputable garden than when I was single ... or when I was pregnant. I read and read and read when I was pregnant with Aubrey. Even now, I compulsively buy books in an effort to *find time to read them.*

Anyway, the book.

It was well-written, but terrible. I was so depressed I wanted to poke my eyeball out with my thumb. *The Time Keeper's Daughter* was truly a drag. It was all about this horrible secret the husband had that ate up his family as a result. All his relationships were altered because of the secret. All of his family suffered. I spent the whole book saying, "If only." Or "Just tell them, dammit!"

And then I wondered about my own secret confusion.

My secret love for Rob. The love I thought I wasn't supposed to have anymore. The one I thought I wasn't supposed to feel anymore.

Paul knew I loved Rob. But did he know how much? Did he know that while I didn't think about Rob everyday, when I *did* think of him it was an aching, haunting love? A furtive one. Like a shameful addiction. A love that created doubt. Doubt in my ability to love Paul fully. It was too horrible to say, let alone think. So I didn't. I got ready for painting class instead.

My painting class was a little unorthodox. Just my style. I drove my car into a muddy alley behind Sundance Natural Foods and muttered to myself about the lack of parking. Once inside the building, I turned down a maze of stark corridors until I got to the workshop's entrance. The room was a little chilly, but the instructor had only just arrived, so the heater hadn't had time to do its job yet.

The work tables were in the center of the room and waist high. Bar stools surrounded them in no particular order. Art supplies were *everywhere*. In baskets and boxes around the perimeter, under the tables, in corners, on shelves. Glitter, magazine clippings, bookmarks, cards, snake skin, fur, Modge-Podge, glue, and paint. We'd all been given canvasses to work on, but first we had to start our class with reverence and centering.

We gathered around the only carpeted area in the room – the corner next to the bathroom. Some sat on the one sofa present – a futonish thing – some sat on pillows on the floor, and some just on the fluffy rug. One of those rugs that look like you'd skinned a yeti. We were in a circle around a big drum. It had a skin stretched across the top, and our instructor passed out those drum sticks with the covered knob at the end.

We were given a chant to repeat and we all settled into a rhythm of banging the drum and chanting. It seemed to go on forever. I was itching to get to the canvas, but I knew that it was part of the creative process and I needed to be present for this, too. I pounded and chanted, beat and sang. Pretty soon I felt a calmness and a sisterhood wick through my veins. At the end, we closed our eyes and breathed in the power we'd raised and felt our roots push through Mother Earth.

I am guided.
I am guarded.
Guided, guarded, Mother Divine.

"Tonight we are going to paint *growing*," the instructor said.

Growing, birthing, seeds preparing under a tarp of snow white paint.

I spread thick layers of green and mud brown, building roughness. I smeared and swirled the brush on the canvas, creating earth for my ideas to nurture. When I'd gotten the soil down, I picked up a strange tool I'd seen in ceramics classrooms. It had a wooden handle surrounding a silver metal rod with a tiny ball tip ending. The whole thing was shorter than a pencil. I used it to write through the wet paint. Words. Secrets. But mostly things I wanted to grow that year. Abundance. Patience. Love. Self-Assurance. Clarity. I found tools that were designed to add texture and dragged them through the wet paint. When the paint dried, not only would the texture look cool, but I could touch it. I loved feeling things with my fingertips.

I cleaned up my tools and washed my hands. I couldn't do anymore until that layer of paint dried. Thoughts percolated and I stared at the canvas with mistrust. I wanted those things to grow in my life, yes, but – that layering and covering things up smacked of dishonesty. More secrets. I was leery.

I walked away – through the other painters and their quiet murmurs. I pawed through a box of animal spirit cards I found on the studio's altar and drew one at random – The Lynx. I looked up the meaning in the companion book. Card number 18, Lynx, *Secrets*. A shiver went through me and I gritted my teeth. *Fuck*.

I was so tired of feeling the need to tip-toe around Paul. To not let him know that I really really loved Rob and that sometimes my love for Paul paled in comparison. But how could I compare? How could I even *think* that?

I loved Paul. Madly and truly. He held me and loved me and gathered our children together and held down the fort and laughed with me and played silly games with the kids and built collages with us and took me to romantic dinners on my birthday.

Paul was the guy that impulsively bought a yellow house with me after only dating for two months. Paul was the guy that slowly explained Congress stuff to me and paused *West Wing* to tell me what was going on without getting irritated, and watched documentaries with me about food and the environment when he'd rather watch a Mafia crime movie or boxing.

Paul was the guy that held me when I had bad dreams. He was the guy that didn't say anything when I snuck butter on the popcorn at the movies, even though he didn't like eating it himself. He was the guy that didn't laugh at me when I was in earnest, but did when I jumped up and down on the couch.

I loved him because he was willing to act foolish with me and that we had private jokes like: Emil the Tentmaker, and "Edwin, the towels are staring at me." I loved him because he kissed me long and soft and let me sit on his lap. And because my soul creaked and despaired when I imagined a life without him; and when he felt pain, I couldn't breathe.

And that's why I could never say what I was feeling.

My fist clenched under the animal spirit companion book in my lap. Defiant.

CHAPTER 27

𝒫aul and I watched a movie soon after that painting class. *The Last Kiss*. At the end we debated. Ironically, the movie was about secrets. I bubbled inside. My neurons poked me and my soul screamed. Secrets seemed to follow me everywhere. Baiting me. Urging me to tell. Or not – I couldn't really tell what I was supposed to do. I just felt raw and green and broken. Or unbroken, like a wild horse, afraid of humans and knowing, somehow, that to involve myself with them was fraught with danger and pain.

We debated the ending. Should the character have told, or not? I said, 'yes,' remembering *The Time Keeper's Daughter* and the destruction of the family through that one withheld secret. I thought of the Lynx. Paul said, 'no.'

"There was no reason to tell her, except to appease his own guilty conscience. It only hurt her. It was *selfish* of him to tell her." He seemed passionate about it – adamant even – and I swallowed my words. I had almost made up my mind to tell him right then.

Would it be selfish of me to say anything? It would most certainly hurt him. There really wasn't any purpose but to get it off my chest. Paul went to the bathroom to brush his teeth. I stared at the poster at the foot of our bed. It was a replica of a painting of a sculptor, who – having fallen in love with his art – found his sculpture had come to life, and reciprocated and responded to his love. In the painting, she had reached down and was kissing her sculptor. It was a moving painting that held meaning for me. To be that in love! So in love that you could bring something inanimate to life. Did I love Paul that much? Did I love Rob that much? Did I *still* love Rob that much?

Questions haunted and hurt.

Paul walked back into the bedroom.

"What?" he said. "Are you alright?"

I blinked. I looked at him, and then looked away.

"Just thinking about the movie." I looked back at the poster and the passion there. Could I have that passion for Paul again? I did when we first got together. And it had come and gone through the years. As was normal. All relationships were like that. We talked, we reconnected, and we rekindled. But the times in between seemed so forlorn, I wondered if it were normal.

I remembered lamenting to my mom one day on a weekend visit.

"What if I'm not supposed to be in this relationship? What if I'm supposed to be with someone else? My love for Rob felt so different."

"Do you really think that being with someone else would feel different than this?" my mom had asked.

I doodled on the notepad in my lap and bit my lower lip, trying not to cry. My mom and I sat across from each other at either ends of the couch, the arms of the couch at our backs.

"No. Because none of them would be Rob." I shoved the yellow legal pad from my lap. "I just miss Rob," I had said. And then I had bitten my palm.

Now the poster taunted me. Urging me to talk to Paul, to tell him my fears. My fears that I didn't love Paul as much as I loved Rob and that once I told Paul, he'd not want to be with me anymore.

Who would stay for *that*?

"Just thinking about the movie," I said, "and the secrets." I looked down at the feather comforter on our bed. The duvet cover was a waffled cotton that buttoned up like a sweater.

"Do you *really* believe that if you have a secret that would quite possibly hurt the other party by knowing it, you shouldn't tell?" He stopped his approach to the side of the bed.

"Why?" he asked. His tone implied a bittersweet mixture of suspicion and compassion.

"Because I have one," I blurted. "And it won't affect our lives if you know it. It won't change anything. And it would hurt you to know it. The only purpose to tell it, would be to get it off my chest."

He sat beside me on the bed and put his hand on my leg.

"Tell me."

I shook my head.

"I'm afraid," I said.

"Whatever it is, we'll work it out. I can't help you if I don't know what it is."

"You can't fix it. There's nothing to fix." I started crying and he pulled me up to a seated position. The better to hold and rock me.

"Give me a day or two to figure out how to say it," I said, after I had control of my voice.

THE FOLLOWING WEEK I WALKED INTO THE PAINTING STUDIO AND SAT down at the bar stool in front of my canvas. The brown and green mud paint was hard by then and the texture I'd built in reminded me of cracks in the earth after a hot summer. I saw my words, my wishes and my affirmations drawn into the earth – solid.

And then. I covered it all. With white paint. Everything. Snowed in.

I hoped that the seeds I planted underneath would germinate.

That the birthing process wouldn't be too painful.

I made a wintry scene and added texture wherever I could. Snake skin, sheep's wool, leather, beads, feathers, leaves, a lone burgundy-colored ribbon and scratchings through the paint here and there all coalesced into the shape of a mandala.

But I needed more words.

When the paint dried, I found a calligraphy marker and tucked in words and hidden meanings to the pictures I'd painted, drawn or Modge-Podged on from cards.

And then it was done.

I WENT HOME AND WROTE A LETTER TO PAUL. BECAUSE WHEN IT WAS all said and done, it was how I best communicated. It was what I was comfortable with. I would be there after he'd read it to hug him, cry with him, hold his hand, apologize over and over, or talk. But I had to write it out first so that I could get it all out and I wouldn't forget to say something important.

It was the hardest letter I'd ever written and I went through myriads of drafts before I settled on one. I handed it to him. He was sitting on the living room sofa and the children were in bed.

"I'll be in the bedroom. Come to me when you're ready," I said.

Would he stay with me after reading it? I wouldn't blame him if he didn't.

> Dear Paul.
> I don't know how to say such a wicked thing, so I'll just say it. I don't love you as much as I did Rob. Both then *and* even now. It hurts me to say that, or to feel it, or believe that it's true. And I ache for the pain it must now cause you.
>
> I know I shouldn't compare my love for the two of you, but I don't know how else to judge for myself the depth of my love for you.
>
> Some believe that you only have one soulmate and that once you've had that and it's gone, for

whatever reason, the other loves you have are not as intense, shadows of the real thing. I don't know if that's true. It sounds bleak – that we'd only get one.

You were right about when we got married. You said I wanted something magical to happen and I did – though I wasn't aware of it at the time. I wanted to love you more. I wanted the sick, dead, broken feeling to go away.

Once upon a time I was so much in love with you. I knew that if Rob showed up mysteriously alive (like in *Castaway*) that I wouldn't want to go to him, but rather to stay with you. *You* were where my heart lived. And then it changed.

Remember that night in the yellow house after we'd only been living together for a few months, when you said that you had no intention of marrying me? That you loved me and were committed to me, but that you didn't need a piece of paper from the government telling you that? Remember that I slept on the couch that night?

As corny as it sounds, when you said that, my heart broke and I put up a wall. Maybe even the same one I had when Rob died. It certainly felt like a death – a death of a relationship – or a love. A hope. A dream. And so now with that wall up that keeps the bad hurts out, I've kept the good feelings from being felt as well. My love for you. Since that day I've not had the same love for you as I did before you said that fateful thing.

I thought that if we got married that broken love would heal and it would be like it was before you said you didn't want to marry me. I thought that if I could shed Rob's name (Gomes-Pereira) I'd love him less and you more. I'd grieve less and move on.

But just the fact that you were only marrying me to make me feel better should've alerted me that I was even subconsciously looking for something you couldn't give me.

It's true that I'm unhappy but I won't be any happier away from you. With this wall up I won't love anyone. It won't do any good to run from this – the walls would come with me.

I think once the wall comes down I can love again – I can love you like I did before.

But what if I can't? I'm afraid. What am I here for? If not for love? And if my love for you is only a shadow of what it used to be – why would you stay? You are worth more than that.

Maybe this has nothing to do with Rob. Maybe this is just about the power of my love – what I know it's capable of – and a broken heart that's never healed.

Or maybe it is none of this – and it's only depression talking.

I **do** love you. But it doesn't feel whole. And is that fair to either of us? You didn't count on this baggage from me, and I didn't count on trying for love after another had been brutally torn from me.

I hope for us,
Love,
Valerie

PAUL WALKED IN AND SAT ON THE BED. I PUT DOWN MY BOOK. I looked at his caring eyes. He put his hand in mine and said three words.

"Don't be stupid."

He pulled me to him and I held my breath. And then I choked and gasped and my heart pounded and I believed.

It was okay.

It was okay to love Rob.

Paul was okay with it.

I didn't have to hide it like a skanky drug addiction.

I could accept whole parts of myself that I'd been denying were real.

Don't be stupid.

And then I laughed.

And then the wall crumbled a little bit.

EPILOGUE

AUGUST 2010

I wish the grass here was lush and silky. I want to swim my arms and legs through it like I do in my sheets when I first wake up on Sunday mornings. But the grass is brown and pokey underneath my belly where my tee-shirt rides up and on the underside of my arms.

I'm lying on top of Rob's grave anyway.

But I don't swim in it. Instead I close my eyes and listen to the wind rustle the trees and hear the birds. I hear car engines, too, from the nearby roads, but I pretend they are wind.

I was hoping there wouldn't be anybody around so that I could talk openly to Rob, though I only have to turn my mind to him and we can converse the other way. The wind snares madly at the trees in consent.

But there are people here, planting flowers four graves down.

The wind is madly hopping from tree to tree, ruffling the pages of my journal and my hair. Smiling, I wonder what Rob is trying to say. And why – if he is trying to say something – he's not communicating in my mind – as was our custom years ago.

You won't listen to me now, he teases. *You're writing and not turning your mind to me.*

Do you have something of import to say?

No. Only that I'm always here for you. Forever. Through good times and bad.

The wind slows to caress my cheeks, then ruffles again in laughter.

And I think of Paul, who promises those things, too.

Being in Massachusetts is weird now. We drove to a park in Rhode Island yesterday and I felt sick with Fernanda driving. Not carsick, but sick with worry and fear. She drives too close to cars and doesn't lift her foot from the gas pedal when the car in front of us brakes. And I realized today that I was afraid we'd crash. Even when *I* drive here, my hands are clasped around the wheel and my shoulders are tense and the teeth in my mouth ache from clenching.

For years, when Aubrey was younger, I didn't want anyone but me driving her anywhere. Her first field trip on a bus was traumatic for me.

I like lying on my back on Rob's grave. It feels oddly comforting, as if I'm snuggling with him. On the way here to the cemetery I saw a young man walking down the road and his facial features reminded me of Rob.

I've seen other men through the years that have looked like Rob, but only one who made me look more than once.

It was in a group of people outside waiting for my stepdaughter to get out of school. He was turned away from me with a young girl in pink at his side. His hands on his hips, the way his shorts fell, and his hair cut all paralyzed me. I stared at his back for two minutes but never had the courage to call attention to myself and seek out his face.

The first time I brought Aubrey to Rob's grave after we'd moved away to Oregon, she picked up a rock and handed it to me. I had picked one up, too. But she hadn't seen me do it.

I kept them both for a few years, until they disappeared one time while going through his box of things. The stones' import was forgotten, I suppose, because I don't have them now.

(GRIEF TIP #1,413: Always label everything even though you

know there's no way you could forget the significance of one of your treasures.)

Why do I keep coming to Massachusetts? I feel useless and disoriented, but I already know the answer.

To remember little tidbits I forget back home. I travel here as pilgrimage to never forget.

To forge a bond between the cousins in case it's needed later on when the children are older and they want a friend that remembers them from back when. Or if anything ever happened to Paul and me, the kids would come here, and Zoe and Nora would become their sisters. Insurance against them being strangers if that were ever to transpire. These are all my reasons.

Is that cold? Selfish?

I feel floaty and restless.

I want to cry here, at his grave, like a true widow. But, despite actually being one, so much of what I think widows are, come from books and movies. And the truth is, I *have* felt like crying here – even twice on the way to the gravesite – but I stopped them, the tears, to save them for the cemetery. Isn't that stupid?

The ground is hard, but I don't want to get up from Rob yet – like he's sleeping next to me. I wonder if he'd like me now. Maybe. Some of me has changed (I think even Fernanda notices my growing confidence) and my parts of color are more pronounced. That might be likable to him. Or not.

I imagine texting Paul.

At the grave.
Wanna say anything to Rob?

But I already know the answer.

Thank you.

As strange as that may seem to others, I understand this perfectly.

> I'm sorry you died – but because you did – thank you. Thank you for my wife. Thank you for helping her become the woman she is now. I never would've had her in my life except for you – so thank you.

And now I tear up. But I don't know why. Because of the beauty in Paul's soul? Because I love Paul and *I thank Rob, too*? Or cry because of Rob's death -- and that it feels creepy to thank him for dying?

The wind whips up again and I take deep breaths … I allow the love of the universe to fill me up. A mantra. It works and I feel calmer.

I've collected a little yellow stone from beneath me that reminds me of the sidewalk chalk Joey was playing with two days ago.

I wonder what Rob's casket looks like now?

It's odd. When I get up to leave, I find I can't. Not yet, for some reason. I wait to see if I can know.

I like sitting here. It's the first time in ten years I've allowed myself the time to just sit and write or rest while here. Usually it's just a quick duty call of sorts. Something I do before leaving Massachusetts.

I've always wanted a place to visit him in Oregon. I planted a pear tree (that's what Rob told me Pereira – our last name – meant) in Oregon at my first house, but moved soon after. It died under the first renters' care. I planted another one just this spring – many years later – still with that wish to have an Oregon monument of sorts to visit. The dog ate the damn tree.

I was beginning to think I wasn't *meant* to have a place to grieve, that I must always carry my conversations with me instead of bringing them to his gravesite (or proxy site.) But then weeks later little sprouts of leaves had poked out of that seemingly dead, and definitely violated, stick in the ground. There were no branches, just leaves sticking out of the teeny dwarf variety trunk. The leaves started all the way at the ground. So funny and awkward looking – but determined and proud.

The wind calls again and I wonder if Rob helped those leaves to grow – to remind me not to give up hope. That remembering him and loving him still, after all this time, is not wrong. And that loving *Paul* is not wrong and that, perhaps, Rob is saying thank you, too. To Paul. For loving me and bringing me back to life – and love.

Thank you, Rob.

AUTHOR'S NOTE

When I first sat down to write this book, I struggled. A lot. Mostly because going back and re-thinking the past doesn't work for me. In fact, I tried really hard to stay in the present because I usually thought five years ahead. But here I was, wanting to go back, but afraid to at the same time.

On August 17, 2000 – thirteen years ago – my husband died. Being twenty-six and newly pregnant complicated my grief, and in some ways I felt like I didn't even start mourning him until after my son was born. I knew at that point I wanted to write about my experience – my journey through grief. I wanted others in my place to not feel so alone in their world when they read my words. And also I knew something about the cathartic and healing power of writing, having journaled for years. So I was committed to writing about that time and tried, however, without success for more than eight years.

At first my grief was too raw. I spent my days staring at the living room wall, and – when I did go out – avoided friendly strangers at checkout counters and swim classes, people who didn't know he was gone and asked about him. I called credit card companies to cancel his cards and gave away some of his

AUTHOR'S NOTE

clothes. But I couldn't throw away his toothbrush or the pregnancy test stick I'd peed on that evening before he died.

I couldn't write about it then, so I waited and tried again later.

I tried again when I'd moved out of state and bought a new house. I purged my emotions into wet clay vessels, and my roommate watched my then two-year-old daughter and six month old son while I ran around and around the block in my Saucony sneakers. I watched the sun flash out from behind trees and counted the seams in the sidewalk. The air was nippy and I composed words to write later.

But later was always later. The words, when I wrote them, weren't what I wanted. They didn't express how I found myself holding my breath for no particular reason. They didn't articulate how it ached when I had to call my mom to tell of my infant's first laughter because I couldn't tell my husband.

And then I fictionalized it. And a door opened. I wrote of someone else's pain and mine lessened somehow. But I wanted to tell my story, so I stopped because it was fiction.

I needed to begin again. It was time. Time to write our story. But I had to go back to do that. I needed to re-open the wounds and examine the pain in all its concrete sensory detail. And I was afraid.

I was afraid of the pain that I knew must accompany that trek. Afraid of how I'd be with my family while I was excavating my memories. Who would care for my children while I was in the past? Who would be a companion to the man I was married to now? Wouldn't it hurt him to see me crying over Rob – the one I never left, but the one who left me with his death? How would me going back to Before affect my relationships in Now? Would it threaten the serenity and happiness we had?

My two year old is fifteen now. She's learning Japanese, stays up too late at night reading, and draws when she wants to express herself or be alone. She plays Dungeons and Dragons twice a week, is in art school, and is teaching herself how to play the piano. She often sports blue hair, fedoras, and all things black.

AUTHOR'S NOTE

The baby I found out I was pregnant with, the night before Rob died, is twelve now. He's analytical, compassionate, and has a great sense of humor. He loves computer games, making up his own role-playing games, and Legos. He hates people who litter, loud noises and trying new foods.

They both like Doctor Who, anime, and World of Warcraft.

The man my children call "Dad" fed my son formula in bottles, changed his diapers and played "Tickle Monster" with him. He cradled my daughter in his lap when she was little and read to her at night and they both called him "Big Hairy Guy" for laughs.

So, would it be worth it to go back? Could it shatter the 'Now'? Those questions plagued me and stunted my writing. I couldn't even start.

This is perhaps why I had not written the story before now. The potential for hurting the people that I cared about was so monumentally in front of me.

Because what would happen was this: I'd remember a flash of memory and go to write it down. While I was there I'd fester and cling to shards of recollection and agonize over not the way things used to be but the things that would never be. And this was where the present got tricky. How did I stay pleased with my life and my new marriage while I lamented over my dead husband never walking my daughter down the aisle at her wedding?

And then digressions bled through that had nothing to do with anything. Like, I struggled over saying "my" daughter. I wanted to say "his" daughter. But then flashed to "our" daughter. But that couldn't be right because the man I'm with now – the one that has raised her since she was three years old – has adopted her. So she's our daughter – his and mine. Not my late husband's. Not anymore. But how could I say that?

Even now I have to ask: Where does he go in my life now? Where can he fit? He must be allowed to stay in some form.

And so he does. A black and white photo of him feeding my infant daughter hangs on our upstairs wall; a flower he gave me

AUTHOR'S NOTE

and I pressed long ago is framed and holds a place on our living room altar; and he lives on in my journal, my dreams and my memories. And that is enough. It has to be.

Sometimes the children and I would light a candle on his birthday and sing for him, but I'd glance over at my current husband and often wonder what he thought about when we did this.

And so I was afraid to go back.

But I had to.

So now that I've finished the book, I feel like an epic section of my life is over. I still have days where I miss Rob. In fact, I just went to the Azores on a recent vacation (a place he had visited as a teenager and still had family living there) and I got teary-eyed thinking how I wished we could've gone there together; or when I went in one of Lisbon's huge cathedrals during that same vacation, I lit a candle for him and cried, knowing he would've loved seeing it.

But despite the 'grief' days -- which aren't overwhelming or, honestly, very often anymore (a statement which at one time I would've been loath to say) -- my life is rich and full.

I remember him with fondness and love. I cry at movies when the husband dies. I tell my kids stories about him. I write about him. I dream about him. We talk to his mom every week by phone, and we fly to visit her every summer. He is still very much in our lives and sometimes we still cry about him, but those times are fewer and fewer between. Mostly we love him and remember him during unique anniversaries or birthdays, and at Dias de los Muertos we build him a special altar in his honor.

It didn't hurt those around me to write this book.

Maybe it even brought us closer.

~ August 2013

READER'S GUIDE

1. How would *you* go on after the death of a spouse (or brother, or mother)?
2. What's the scariest part for you in the *moving on, letting go, but not* part of grieving?
3. Did you find Valerie's lack of outward emotion off-putting?
4. What was your opinion of Valerie's move across the country? Was it warranted? Was it selfish? What would you have done?
5. What were the most touching parts of the book for you?
6. What death have you survived? (It doesn't have to be a person. It can be a death of a dream, hope, job, *et cetera*.)
7. Do you think that internet dating is a valuable tool in today's society?

ACKNOWLEDGMENTS

This book took so many years to write that I'd almost given up. Thank you to Nawaz for encouraging me to get it finished. Thanks to Paul for encouraging me to write, period. Thanks to my critique group for hearing three years of drafts: Anna, Mike, Brittany, Terry, Tiffany, Darryl Lynne, Ann, Jamie, Susan, Julie, and sometimes Jesse and Tamathy. Thanks to my beta readers: Ali, Deanna, and David. Thanks to those of you that agreed to write blurbs and reviews.

Thanks to Tamara Leroy of Candor Designs for my webpage and author photo. And thanks to Maddie Whitmarsh for editing, Ali Ozgenc for the cover design, and Patricia Marshall at Luminare Press for interior layout.

And thank you to Debi Gliori for writing the book *No Matter What*, and letting me quote it in this memoir.

I'm so grateful for all of you.

HOW TO GRIEVE

EVEN WHEN YOU DON'T WANT TO

Valerie Ihsan

WILLOW BENCH BOOKS
SPRINGFIELD, OREGON

How to Grieve

When I was 26, I told my husband, Rob, we were finally pregnant with our second child. We'd been trying for eight months. Later that same day, Rob died. He'd fallen asleep driving and hit a highway signpost.

I was pregnant and was now a widow. I had a 22-month-old daughter.

I didn't know how to be a widow. I didn't know any widows. I had no road map, no blueprints. There was no how-to guide--and prior to 9/11 there weren't many books on grieving a spouse at such a young age.

Let this booklet be that guide for you.

(Certified Bereavement Facilitator since 2004; Widow since 2000.)

AFTERWARDS

*A*fter you've heard the news, everything is a normal reaction. You could cry, scream, stare at the wall, rock yourself, eat, or throw up. It's all normal. There's no one right way to grieve.

LET SOMEONE KNOW. Let your family/friends/neighbors help you. You can't do this alone. Most likely someone else will pick up the reins at this point and finish notifying whoever needs knowing. Food will materialize. Your house chores will start being done by others, and you can continue to stare at the wall. That's what I did. I cried, too, but mostly I just sat. And waited. For whatever was going to happen next.

MAKE ONLY IMMEDIATE DECISIONS. There'll be plenty of other little things you'll be called upon to deal with. Don't worry about the long-term stuff right now. The mainstream advice is not to make any major decisions right after a tragedy. Sometimes it can't be helped—like approving an organ transplant, or needing to move out of the rental house that you can no longer afford on one salary—but put off whatever you can. I was fortunate enough to not have to decide anything at first, except choosing his casket and answering funeral/wake related questions.

Your head and heart are so full of other things, you aren't in your right mind. How can you make a major life decision at this time? I did move after my husband died, but I waited six months before deciding and then made it happen in the following two. Part of my hurry was my pregnancy. I wanted to be settled before I gave birth. But I still staged it so that there were built-in chunks of time where I could stop and re-assess. And I had family helping me through the process.

For instance, when I moved to Oregon, I moved into an apartment—that my mother secured for me—knowing I wanted to purchase a house. I didn't want to hurry through the process of figuring out what would work best for my family's needs. Staying in the apartment for five months allowed me to settle in and breathe, give birth to my son, get used to living by myself (with children), and slowly look at houses.

Those other little things that pop up will seem so insignificant that you'll be pissed you're being asked to deal with them. How dare I have a college final a week after my husband dies? How dare I have a dental appointment right now? How dare I have a pre-cancerous mole I need to have removed twelve days after I've buried my best friend?

All three of those examples were ones I dealt with within three weeks of my husband's death. Yours will be different. Perhaps you'll have to give a presentation at work, or fire a care-giver. Sometimes it just can't be postponed and you muddle through it as best as you can.

GIFTING. You'll be approached by family and friends asking for something to help them remember your loved one. A shirt. A picture. A lunch box. Whatever. Others are grieving, too. And sometimes the request won't come out so well. It might feel greedy to you, or insincere. Or maybe you'll just panic at the thought of giving something away that was your beloved's. Most likely you'll have a heart-felt request for some small token, and they'll make it clear that you needn't bother with it until you are ready.

I, personally, gifted out Army pins, clothes, cuts of cloth (when more than one person wanted the same favorite flannel shirt), a Boston Bruins coat, and the head of a hockey stick.

YOU'LL HAVE VISITORS. But don't feel you have to entertain. Let them do for you. Ask for help, if you can. Otherwise, just let them be in the same room with you. They want to be helpful and they might not know how, so let them sit with you and not talk, or let them cry with you. Both can be cathartic.

AT HOME AND WORK

*E*MPLOYMENT/PAPERWORK. When I decided to quit my job after Rob died, my boss was genuinely confused. She thought it was best to keep busy when grieving. And so it is, for some. But truth be told, I was busy. So busy. At home I had a toddler, a pregnancy, doctor's appointments, calling creditors to cancel credit cards, and applying for death benefits from the Social Security office, the V.A., and my husband's place of business. I needed to get his things from work, I needed to invest the life insurance money I fortunately received, and I needed to sleep and grieve. It was all exhausting. I didn't have the time or energy for a job.

Unfortunately, some grieving spouses don't have this luxury, and some, I'm sorry to say, need to now get two jobs to fill the gap. If this is the case for you, please, seek as much assistance as possible from government programs, family, and friends. Again, you don't have to do this alone. It's best for all if you don't.

RELIGION/SPIRITUALITY. There is a great deal of variety here, and so much room for exploration. Some find refuge and comfort in their church or religion; some lose their faith and leave it. As time passes, you might find yourself wanting to explore or practice a different religion or spiritual way of life. If you do, this is normal, too. After all, we are not the same as we were before our tragedy. The religion of my childhood couldn't serve me after my husband's death, so I explored other beliefs and found the right avenue for myself.

Some might feel threatened by your exploration, but this is your grief journey—a personal and private matter for you. Don't let others bully you in, or out, of what you feel is right for you at this horrible time in your life. You are in charge. Even if it doesn't feel like it.

TELLING THE CHILDREN. This was terrifying for me. And it's tricky. It depends greatly on the age of the child. Different age groups have different cognitive abilities and needs, and require different communication from us. You must be careful what you say. Children are very literal-minded.

You don't want to say that the deceased love one is sleeping, because the child will continue to wait for them to wake up, or worse, not want to go to sleep themselves for fear of never waking up again.

And what if you say they've gone to heaven, and then they want to die so they can go to heaven, too? I was so worried about saying the wrong thing to my two-year-old daughter and scarring her for life. How do you tell your toddler that her daddy is dead?

Ultimately, I think you have to listen to your gut and then run it by someone else first. Talk to people who are familiar with this. Consult a counselor, a grieving expert, or other parents that are widows, or widowers.

This is how I did it:

I used Debi Gliori's picture book No Matter What. There is a passage that talks about love being like the stars that are far, far away. That the stars are still there even when you can't see them. I told my daughter that Daddy was far, far away like the stars, and that he couldn't come home, but that he'd love us forever—no matter what.

WHEN THE KIDS ARE GRIEVING. Of course my unborn son wouldn't grieve the loss of someone he didn't even know. It turns out though, that (later) kids in this situation sometimes do—grieve the loss of never having met a person they are so intimately connected with. Also, sometimes wee small ones just pick up on our sadness and grief, and will act out their own response to that.

I thought my daughter would be too young to remember her father and therefore wouldn't have the pain associated with grief, but about a year after Rob's death, she started saying she missed him. This was especially challenging for me because I was just hitting the 'Moving-on' stage and I was afraid that her outward mourning would set me back. I asked a therapist at that time if she thought my daughter needed counseling.

"No. Missing him is an appropriate behavior."

At three years old, she must have reached the cognitive ability to process out loud and talk about him. When she'd say, "I miss Daddy," I'd say, "Me, too," and she'd hug me and then be off to her next thing. That's all she wanted—a few extra minutes to say what she was feeling, and to be acknowledged for it. Perhaps that's all any of us want.

If your children are older, nine or twelve, say, then family counseling might be an excellent choice. There are many websites and other resources that outline (by age) what we can do to support our grieving children, such as answering questions clearly and honestly, and avoiding phrases like: "God took him," "He's gone to a better place,' or "She's sleeping in death now".

Please see the Resource page in this booklet.

REACHING OUT

WRITE IT DOWN/JOURNALING. I have always been a journaler. But now I found it imperative. I needed to capture every memory I could think of and write it down. For me, for my children. And writing helped me organize my thoughts and feelings. Here are some other things that journaling can offer: a place to pour out the sorrow and venom, to remember, and to worry. And it was a place to recall the special moments that perhaps I'd taken for granted before, but was now so grateful that they'd happened.

I wrote every day. Several times a day. Sometimes I wrote letters: to my late husband, to my daughter, to my unborn child, to God, or to my angels/spirits/guides. Sometimes I had conversations in my journals. Mostly I just wrote about my emotional state. Getting fears and anxieties out of my head and on to paper was most therapeutic. Something about using my hands and processing feelings at the same time.

Journal writing was a lifeline for me—perhaps because I was a Blended griever. (See below in "Grieving Types.")

FINDING A MENTOR OR SUPPORT SYSTEM. You may

feel that you already have a support system with your family and friends, and if you do, I'm so happy for you. You may feel that you don't need or want a counselor, or a support group. And you may be absolutely right in that.

Or you might not be.

I tried a couple of different things. I ate dinner at my sister-in-law's house so I didn't need to be alone on weekday nights; I visited my friends on the weekends when they were home from work; and I attended a grief support group a couple of times. My friends were helpful, the support group wasn't. For me.

I want to stress that I think support groups are great. And I sort-of wish I'd continued going, or gone later, but with only three months between me and the death, I just didn't want to talk to a room full of strangers. And honestly, it didn't occur to me to find a counselor. But I did need something.

I found my something quite serendipitously. She was on a bulletin board. In the form of a brochure on stress-relieving meditation. She was a certified bereavement facilitator whose baby girl had died. This woman became part of my tribe.

I started seeing her once a week, and that was where my healing really began.

So don't immediately discount a third party mentor or support group. They really can do wonders for you. And if you try it and you don't feel a connection to your new therapist or grief support group, try another one. And maybe one more.

However, it is important to note that some people are not emotional grievers. They don't feel comfortable talking their feelings out. Maybe you are one of these. Perhaps you'd rather plant a flower garden in memory of your loved one, or paint a fence. If you are an active griever—someone that needs to do something physically to work through grief—these can be ways to process your emotions.

Every expression of grief is the right one. One book that made this so clear to me was I'm Grieving As Fast As I Can by Linda Feinberg. There are hundreds of accounts from young widows and widowers in such varied circumstances that they had to all grieve in different ways. Read it. You might just feel better.

GRIEVING TYPES. In Dr. Kenneth Doka's book, Disenfranchised Grief, he describes four types of grievers: Intuitive, Instrumental, Blended, Dissonant.

Intuitive types are the ones with the outward emotions. They cry, feel exhausted and anxious, and/or have bouts of confusion.

Instrumental grievers are the ones compelled to Do Do Do. They don't particularly care for sharing their feelings and often just want to hurry up and "get better," as if grieving were an illness. These types of grievers could write letters, or train for a marathon to raise money for an organization that researches the type of disease that claimed their loved one. Perhaps they start a foundation. Or make a memory book.

Blended ones are—you guessed it—a combination of both. (And why I think journaling worked so great for me. I got to talk about my emotions...with my hands!)

Lastly, dissonant grievers are in conflict with their grieving style. Maybe they want to cry openly and tell their story but they are in a community or culture that frowns on it, so they hold it in. We sometimes see this in men in North America, and I've been told that the only safe place to cry in Asian countries, is in a movie theater. Or the opposite: dissonant grievers might not be crying and feel like they should—feeling like they're being judged for not reacting properly to the death.

There is no one right way to grieve. Knowing what kind of griever you are may help you find some relief.

TELLING EVERYONE ELSE. Somehow all my family just seemed to know about Rob's death. I didn't have to tell anyone except my mom. Other than that, it took me months to tell anyone else. Running into marginal acquaintances or colleagues, or strangers at the YMCA or grocery store, didn't elicit any need on my part to randomly share my story with them. Three months after the fact, I did telephone our best man. I said what I had to say and hung up as fast as I could. I felt he should know, but I didn't feel comfortable chit-chatting with him about it afterwards. And that's okay.

You can do either. Or neither. If you want someone to know that a death has occurred, but you don't feel like handling it yourself, there is no shame in requesting assistance. The best approach is the direct one: "I think Bryan should know. Will you call and tell him? I'm just not up to it." People want to help.

LEARNING NEW THINGS. Without the expected companionship you are used to, you may find yourself with some extra time on your hands. Or maybe you feel busy, but your curiosity has returned. You might start reading books about reincarnation and jet fighter pilots, or take classes in permaculture design.

I was relieved when I started showing signs like these. One of my fears was that I'd never regain a zest for life. When I started reading again, I knew I was safe from that.

CARRYING ON

FINDING NEW FRIENDS AND LETTING GO OF OLD ONES. As if we didn't already have enough trauma in our lives right now, relationships with friends can change, too. Sometimes they can't be there for you during this time. Don't take it personally. And don't write them off. They're just grieving at a different rate than you are, or in a different way.

Grief changes relationships. It's unavoidable. Before the death, your friends related to you as a couple; now they don't. You definitely can lose your sense of self during this time. (Who am I now without my partner?) You will learn a lot about people through this process. Most of all, yourself.

Often other friends will step in when you least expect it to fill the void. Any desire to readjust who your friends are, and who you spend your time with, indicates a newfound inner strength. And that is always a cause for celebration.

C.A.M. CARE. COMPLEMENTARY ALTERNATIVE MEDICINE IS A WAY to nurture and take care of yourself. If your pocketbook allows it, try to receive some sort of preventative alternative therapy that brings you peace or pleasure once a week. And then adjust accordingly.

CAM refers to things like: acupuncture, Reiki, massage, emotional processing techniques, or other energy or body work. These are both helpful and healthful to you--physically, energetically, mentally, and emotionally. But CAM also includes other things that you can do to support yourself. Maybe that would be: a new bouquet of flowers for the kitchen table, a pedicure, or a month's supply of vitamins and supplements to keep your strength up. A writing retreat to France's cafes and bridges? Yes, please. Emotional R&R for sure.

More traditional care methods might be: lighting a candle at church every week, spending more time with relatives and friends, or quiet time in your garden or a favorite park.

My combination of CAM care was to receive relaxation massages every three weeks, get a pedicure once a month, and learning how to do Reiki on myself. I also promised myself an ocean cruise as soon as my baby was a year old. Which I took.

FEAR. I was always scared after Rob died. I spent months of worry about: physical safety (Who would save me if someone broke into the house at night?), spiritual safety (unreasonable fear of evil spirits attacking me), financial safety (What if I made a bad investment?), and the constant fear of something happening to my children or to myself—either going through another death, or leaving my children orphans.

Fear is normal, too. Try a visualization exercise of meeting Fear and seeing what it looks like. Talk to Fear. Whose face does it have? What does Fear gain by being in your life? What do you gain? Have a conversation. Sometimes that's all that needs to happen to get clarity. If it's too much, talk to someone.

Other more practical things you can do to alleviate some of your fears might be: getting AAA for roadside assistance in case of break-downs on dark nights; writing a will—with godparents for your children; adding a security system to your home; getting a dog.

AND BEYOND

THE FIRSTS. The first birthday without their dad. The first Halloween. The first Thanksgiving. The first Christmas. A bumpy ride for sure, but here's what helps: (1) Have a plan for the day. There will be less stress if you know what to expect from the event, and what part you are playing that day. For instance, "I will show up on time with my special baked beans, stay for two hours, and then leave. While I'm there I will play two card games and eat dinner." (2) Acknowledge that there's someone missing, and that it's weird and sad, and then carry on with the holiday anyway. This can be as simple as raising a glass before a special family meal and saying, "I just want to say that it's really terrible that Rob isn't with us today, but that I'm so thankful that you all are." (3) Mark the event somehow. Create a ritual. Sing happy birthday to the one that's died. Journal about the day without them. Make a photo album of all the pictures you have of your loved one and give a copy to close family members.

ONE YEAR ANNIVERSARY. This is a doozy. The biggest of all the Firsts. As it happened, I was in the very best place for myself (geographically and socially) when the one year anniversary of Rob's death occurred. I was traveling to see family. This gave me a physical action with which to keep myself busy—traveling with very small children is a special kind of busy—and the opportunity to take some private time to acknowledge what day it was. I did this with journaling. After a day with my family, I carved out some time to sit in the backyard and journal. I lit candles and stayed outside until—one by one—tthe flames all went out.

STARTING AFRESH. This will happen at different times for everyone. There is no one right time to be "over" it. The reality is that you are never over it. There will probably always be soft longings, what ifs, or if onlys that can remain. But, dang! our society sure wants it that way. We only get three days of bereavement leave from work (and that's only if you are directly related to the deceased—my mother had to use vacation days to visit me, and my brothers-in-law only had one day off). We are often told we are "doing well" if we aren't showing any emotion. If we confess how horrible we actually feel inside, people are confused. "But I thought you were feeling better." As if grief were something to hurry up and get over.

Believe me. Most grieving people don't want to wallow in grief. It hurts. It makes you feel stupid, slow. You don't fit in anymore. Nothing makes sense anymore. If grieving were something we could just hurry up and get over with, we'd totally do it.

That being said, sometimes it does just feel like it's time to move on. Usually this is done in small steps. Perhaps you stop visiting the grave so often; maybe you finally scatter the ashes. Or you take off your wedding rings, and throw away his toothbrush.

Or maybe you move to a new state, like I did. (Though I'm not advising this, especially if you have no family or support there.) This can be rejuvenating. But just know that the grief will follow you. It may be less intense, or maybe it'll come out full force. Grief comes and goes as it wants to, as you are able to process it. And that's normal, too.

Around this time you might feel ready to start dating again. Or not. It's totally up to you. Some re-marry within the year; some never marry again. Any version of starting afresh is right and true, as long as you are checking in with yourself and listening to your voice instead of to the multitude of well meaning others.

GRIEF ISN'T ALL THAT EXCITING. Some might think otherwise. And parts of it sure are intense, but other parts of it are just like regular life. You need to take out the trash, so you do. You need to enroll your daughter in pre-school, so you do. Grieving all the while.

Grief hits you at mundane moments. While driving to the mountain to go snowshoeing for the first time—true story—or when seeing his favorite toothpaste at the store, or smelling his aftershave on your dad. Another true story. And grief is often a long drawn out general malaise-y feeling, rather than constant tears. Sometimes it's just numbness and forgetting why you were in a room.

CONTINUING CARE--EVEN A YEAR LATER. When I was first widowed, I looked around for someone to tell me how long it would take me to get through the grief process. (Ha!) I find that laughable now, but then I was totally serious. I gave it a good year. I thought that should handle it. But when a year had passed, and I was still feeling restless and unsettled and lonely and sad—despite "moving on" and starting school again and processing all that I thought I needed to process—I got irritated. I was tired of grieving; it was just so boring. Feeling depressed and miserable all the time just gets lame and uninspiring.

Some of what helped me over the restless boring part was still finding time for things that took me out of my headspace. Pedicures, a pottery class, massages, and jogging. Goals helped, too. I signed up for a marathon. Training and school work gave me something to do. And getting a roommate kept me social and prevented total isolation even if I was just at home in my pajamas. I also got to know the neighbors a little bit. And I started dating. Which was momentous.

EVEN LATER

*D*ATING AGAIN. All I can really say about this with any certainty is: It's personal. Here are some issues that might happen and need to be dealt with:

Someone thinks you are starting too soon, or shouldn't be doing it at all. Do it if you want to. And don't let anyone make you feel like it's too soon, or too late. I moved away so that his family didn't have to watch me go through the process. Sounds a tad drastic, and wasn't the only reason I moved. As I said before, I had support from other family members where I moved, so it wasn't as out of the blue as it may seem. It just so happened that the idea of dating other men while my late husband's family looked on was one of the things I considered when deciding whether to move, or not.

If you do start dating another, you might feel like you are betraying your late spouse. Totally normal. It took me a long time to come to terms with this one. But maybe it won't be an issue for someone else. My mother-in-law loves to say, "Everybody's different."

What to say to your children. Think age-appropriate conversations and explanations. Having "sleep-overs with your friend" might work for your three-year-old, but probably you'll have to have a longer discussion with your twelve-year-old. Some parents discuss everything with their children, others don't. Both are right. This is a parenting matter, as much as a personal matter. That means that you get to decide what's right for you and your children. Not your aunt or cousin. You are the parent.

PARENTING SIDE NOTE: I HEREBY GIVE YOU PERMISSION TO parent your children the best way you can with the circumstances you now live in.

For months I felt like a terrible mother for considering a babysitter for my kids. Our parenting plan (Rob's and mine) consisted of never having anyone watch our kids except a family member or really close friend.

My mother kindly set me straight and said, "You can't hold yourself accountable for keeping that rule you made back then. The circumstances were different. You don't have 70 aunts, uncles, and cousins to watch your kids anymore. You moved. You just do the best you can now."

FOUR YEARS LATER. AT THIS POINT, I FELT I COULD SAFELY SAY I was done grieving. I was in a long-term relationship; I'd become a licensed massage therapist; I'd kept up with my writing. My children were thriving; we had a puppy. But I was mad. Mad that Rob had died, mad that I didn't get to do the things we'd planned to do together, and mad that I'd had to go through the last four years. And I still missed him. I still wished he was alive and that we were together.

I realized in the end that this was okay. It was okay to love both my late husband, and the man I was with. It wasn't a betrayal.

But that was my path. Yours may look different, or take you to a separate place all together.

NEW BAGGAGE. THESE WILL COME AND GO. THOUGH SOME MAY stay forever. They could be things that show up years later. Maybe you see how they are connected to your tragedy but it was weird that they didn't show up right away.

My new baggage includes: worrying about people who don't sleep enough, worrying about people driving when they are tired, having a twinge of fear of someone else driving my kids around town, my kids being out of town without me, being afraid of crashing my car when I drive in Massachusetts, having nightmares about my kids dying.

Mostly I don't dwell on these fears. I chalk them up as new idiosyncrasies.

GRIEF SHADOWS. GRIEF IS CYCLICAL. NOT LINEAR. IT DOESN'T actually go away, like something you cross off on a checklist. This thought used to terrify me—that there would be this ever-present cloud hanging over my fragile state of mind, and that I would snap at any moment. But it's not like that at all. It's more like putting your hands in your pockets on a cold day and finding a leftover object. "Oh, there's my lip balm."

My grief shadows are: pear trees, Camel cigarettes, yellow rocks, seeing someone that resembles Rob, and a certain kind of giggle.

They don't make me sad. They evoke memories. Good ones, sad ones, poignant ones. They don't identify me, but they are a part of who I am now—part of the new me.

RESOURCES

WEBSITES

American Humane Association: the nation's voice for the protection of children & animals--Under the Human-Animal Interaction tab, there is a great article on age-related grieving. It is referencing the death of a pet, but all the information is pertinent to the loss of a human family member. http://www.americanhumane.org/interaction/programs/humane-education/pet-loss/age-based-coping-tips.html It includes what you see in the child's behavior, and ways to respond.

Real Warriors: reach out for help to cope with invisible wounds--This website focuses on soldiers and their families. One article talks about helping children through the loss of a parent. Good stuff. http://www.realwarriors.net/family/children/grieving.php

National Association of School Psychologists has a pdf entitled, Helping Children Cope With Loss, Death, and Grief: Tips for Teachers and Parents. You can find it here: http://www.nasponline.org/resources/crisis_safety/griefwar.pdf

RESOURCES

BOOKS

I'm Grieving As Fast As I Can by Linda Feinberg

Letters To My Husband by Fern Field Brooks

Smell the Blue Sky: young, pregnant, and widowed by Valerie Ihsan

Widows Wear Stilettos: a practical and emotional guide for the young widow by Carole Brody Fleet and Syd Harriet

Love is a Mixed Tape: Life and Loss, One Song at a Time by Rob Sheffield

Planet Widow: A Mother's Story of Navigating a Suddenly Unrecognizable World by Gloria Lenhart

A Widow's Walk: a memoir of 9/11 by Marian Fontana

The Alchemy of Loss: a young widow's transformation by Abigail Carter

Young Widower: A Memoir by John W. Evans

FREE BOOK OFFER

Early Reviews for *The Scent of Apple Tea*

"The story grabbed me right away."

"...a beautiful, very touching and realistic characterization of the mother/daughter bond."

"I loved the ending."

"...beautiful, poignant and very meaningful."

"...fun reading and great local flavor."

Family. Courage. Love.

Kathryn Gordon's cozy rural life falls apart when her adult daughter, Heather, is diagnosed with ovarian cancer. While Kathryn researches alternative cures, including communicating with a dead Scottish ancestor, Heather Gordon makes a heroic journey to Scotland with an ex-boyfriend she still loves.

The Scent of Apple Tea is a story of wanting what you can't have, and finding the courage to live and love the life you're given. If you like reading about strong female protagonists and scenic foreign lands, you'll love Valerie Ihsan's debut contemporary women's fiction novel.

Transport yourself today to the quaint farmlands of Oregon's Willamette Valley and the lush lochs and villages of the Scottish Highlands.

"A lyrical, deep and emotional story; the dynamic...will pull you in and make you think about your own relationships." —Kristen James, *All in My Head*

Go to valerieihsanauthor.com to claim your free book.

Dear Fabulous Reader,

Thanks for reading *Smell the Blue Sky – Young, pregnant, and widowed* ENHANCED edition. I hope you enjoyed it, and that it brought you some peace if you are grieving.

Please help spread the word by writing a review on your favorite online retailer or Goodreads, or telling a few friends about the book.

If you'd like to try out my fiction, please go to my website at valerieihsanauthor.com and receive a free digital copy of *The Scent of Apple Tea*.

Peace,

ABOUT THE AUTHOR

Valerie Ihsan is an award-winning author, freelance editor, and dog-lover living in Springfield, Oregon. She loves olives, chai, and Honey Mama's Lavender Red Rose bars. You can find her on Facebook, Instagram, and valerieihsanauthor.com.

www.ingramcontent.com/pod-product-compliance
Lightning Source LLC
Chambersburg PA
CBHW020609300426
44113CB00007B/576